Yancy, the Youngest Hobo

Betty L. Carter

authorHOUSE®

AuthorHouse™
1663 Liberty Drive, Suite 200
Bloomington, IN 47403
www.authorhouse.com
Phone: 1-800-839-8640

First published by AuthorHouse   11/4/2008

ISBN: 978-1-4389-2776-3 (sc)
ISBN: 978-1-4389-2775-6 (hc)

Library of Congress Control Number: 2008909850

Printed in the United States of America
Bloomington, Indiana

This book is printed on acid-free paper.

Contents

Best Wishes,
Betty L. Carter

Foreward

In the spring of 2007, Mr. Irvin Yancey asked me if I'd agree to write his lifes story. He was eighty four years old and would turn eighty five on June 28th. I was aquainted with him through the local Seniors Citizens Center.

I was in the process of writing a novel that was set during World War II and since Mr. Yancey had served during WWII, I had ask him some time before if he would help me get my facts straight so the book would be true to life. He readily agreed to do so. When I finished the book, he was willing to proof read my fiction story to make sure all the facts were correct. He said he really loved the book.

He caught one date that I had written down that was three days off the mid-war timeline. He was right. I changed it immediately. This gentleman was there and knew exactly what he was talking about.

From all he did to help out at the Seniors Center, I could see that he was a quiet man who was always willing to help anyone in any way he could. If someone missed the Seniors bus, he was always glad to run and pick them up. He worked diligently on jig-saw puzzles and played a mean game of chess or checkers with who ever wanted to play. He enjoyed playing Bingo and even called the numbers when the regular caller wasn't there. In fact, several years before, he and his wife had started the Bingo games with materials they provided. Everyone seemed to really enjoy it then and now, as well.

Mr. Yancey had read all three of my books that I had written before and decided he liked my style of writeing. He ask several times if I'd write his lifes story. He said he had a story to tell. I always told him I'd think about it and let him know. When I agreed to do it, he was excited to think of seeing his life in print.

Immediately after this, the doctors said he had a mass on one lung and after tests of all kinds, they told him he had cancer and only had four to six months to live. He handled that well. He said it wasn't the cancer that would get him anyhow, that was a johnny-come-lately. He said it would be some of the other other ills that he had going on.

I knew Mr. Yancey had led an interesting life because he had fought as a machine gunner in World War II. My third book is Appalachian in nature and about a big family back in the hills of Kentucky during WWII. The two oldest children in the story are boys and one is drafted into the Army, the other one joins the Marines and they both go into the war. It is told from the propective of the ones that are left at home. The boys and their mother write letters to each other.

Mr. Yancey had a wealth of information that he so readily shared for that book.

I just didn't realize what an interesting life he had led even before the war. He started putting his memories on cassette tapes and I began transcribeing them onto the computer. I re-arranged when he had missed something and thought of it later on the tapes. I was excited to hear the tapes and bring the story together. Somehow, his shareing his life with me touched me deeply.

Sometimes, I had questions I needed to ask about something that I didn't understand or that just needed more explanations added to.

He told me to call him at home anytime with any questions I had so I did. He was always pleased to answer any questions I had. We'd talk for a long while, discussing plans for his book. It was an honor to me that he trusted me to write what he wanted said.

I wrote it as close to how he told it as I could. He told me that I knew how to fill in the parts where he had left little things out and say it exactly like he would tell me. It would come together interestingly and be enjoyable to where people would want to read it, he said.

I worked on it for a good while then I printed off what I had written and gave him a copy the third or fourth week of July of 2007. When I saw him at the Seniors Citizens Center on Thursday, August 2nd, he had read it and was very pleased with the copy but said he had left out so much, he had so much more to say. I suggested that we get together and he could add whatever he thought of verbally. I told him I'd write it in my own special shorthand on the copy, that probably only I could read.

He said he'd let me choose the day and then he added, "But don't wait to long, I don't know how long I'll be here."

I noticed he was having some difficultly getting his breath but he had been that way before.

I took him seriously, yes, I did, but since the doctors said that he had four to six months, I thought one week wouldn't make a difference. I planned to get together with him the next week. I waited to long. I waited to long.

On Friday, Mr. Yancey wasn't there and the folks from Hospice came into the Seniors Citizen Center and removed his large oxygen tank. They did not replace it.

My husband Jim, commented, " This cant be good, can it?"

I shook my head. Still I thought there was time.

August 6th, 2007

Tonight I got the shocking news that Mr.Irvin Yancey had passed away today. It sent my head and my heart reeling. From his shareing so much of his lifes story, and from feeling the pain of his young life, I suppose that I sort of adopted him as the father that I lost on February 15, 1974. My heart went out to his family. I was and am so sorry that Mr. Yancey and I didn't get to finish the book together.

At his visitation, I met some of his children and grandchildren. I had already met his wife, Cymbaline, when we first discussed my writing his life story. She graciously invited me into their home and shared photos and memories.

She is willing to help me with the finishing of Mr. Yancey's book. I am so sorry for the families loss, and for the empty chair that greets me at the Seniors Citizen Center. I know that loseing a good friend that I'd so recently gotten aquainted with is small in comparison with his families loss. I can understand how his children feel because I've lost my own dad. However; I can't even begin to understand Mrs. Cymbaline's loss.

Mr. Yancey passed from this life quietly in his sleep.

Some folks don't understand my grief. They just don't realize how deeply Mr. Yancey's life story touched me and what it meant to me that he wanted me to tell his memories. He became a friend. Mr. Yancey **trusted** me to write his story.

He told me often, 'You can do it! I trust you, you can make an interesting story out of it, I know you can. I want you to do some of your drawings, too! You can draw a freight train and smoke coming from the coal car where I hid out and built my fires when I was out hoboing around.'

He'd led such an interesting life that writeing his story was easy, no question about it. His daughter Linda, told me he was very excited about the book. She said it gave him joy to the very end of his life and my writeing it gave him a voice. I'm glad that in some small way, I could do that. I'm ever so glad that I started this project. I only wish, how I wish, that I had started it much sooner. It gave me opportunity to get aquainted with Mr. Irvin Yancey, his lovely wife Cymbaline and his fine family. He will live on in the memories of those who loved him, but he is so sadly missed.

In memory of Mr. Irvin Yancey June 28th, 1922---August 6th, 2007

Chapter 1

Mama

Every man has a story to tell. Every life is different, every story different. This old man setting here before you has a story to tell. Some of it is comical, a whole lot of it is sad, some of it is unbelievable, and some of it is plain old rediculous, believe it or not but I swear to you it is all true. Every word.

First thing I can recollect is summer, 1925. I was born in 1922 in Lennet, Kentucky in the out-skirts of Hazard and McCreary County, but far back as I can remember, is when I was about three and a half years old and we lived at Wallings Creek, Kentucky. I guess we moved around a lot.

My Dad worked in a coal mine there on a coal cutting machine. He had different places to cut so he had to stay till they was all cut and we never knowed what time he'd be a coming in home. But he wanted his supper hot and on the table when he got there and he wanted water hot on the stove for his bath. I don't know how he thought she ort to know when he was a coming in, when he come at all different times but he did. My Mom done the best she could.

One evening, Dad come in from work and the fire had gone out under his bath water. It was cold. He started raising cain with my Mom.

I stood there in my little white gown, wide eyed and staring. Dad grabbed me up and carried me to bed. He was covered up all filthy black with coal dust and got my little white gown black with the rank coal dust. It filled my nostrils, almost choking me, the smell of the coal dust. I didn't understand what had just happened.

Had I done something wrong? I didn't know. I turned my face away to the wall and pretended to fall asleep but sleep was a long time a coming. I just laid there a wondering.....I was afraid it was my fault. Couldn't sleep hardly a-tall. Didn't understand.

Mom tried the best that she knowed how, to keep his supper warm and his water hot till he come in. With six of us kids, that was no easy task. But sure enough, one day it happened again. When Dad come through the door, Mom's face turned white. Oh, no, she realized then that she never put extra wood in the stove to keep the bath water hot. Fire was out in the stove and his bath water cooled, his supper plumb cold. Him and Mom got into a rageing argument.

I was scared and hung onto Mom's dress tail tight as a three and a half year old could. She was expecting another little'n too, although I didn't know it at the time. Dad kept on giving her the devil and then retch behind him in a chifferobe and pulled out a 38 pistol. He leveled it down at Mom's belly and shot her in the stomach. She jerked and fell face forward onto the floor, pulling me down with her.

My little mind reeled with shock. Even a three and a half year old knows when something awful has just happened. I scrambled up to my feet and stared at my mother a laying there in her own blood. She moaned a little. Only time I took my eyes off her was then. I covered my eyes with my trembling hands. Had I somehow done something that Dad didn't like to cause this? Was this my fault? Maybe if I had been a better boy......maybe if me and my brothers didn't argue as much over stupid things.....

I think it was Gertrude come then and grabbed me up and took me to the back room. She was a crying as she hummed me a little out of tune song. No sobs, just silent tears coursing down her cheeks, tracking up her face. She didn't understand any more than me what had just happened. She looked at me so helpless. I latched on to her tight as I could.

She wasn't Mom but she was all I had right now. I held on to her like I would never let go. I buried my face in her shoulder but I could still see Mom a laying there in my minds eye, clear as day. That vision would never go away.

Somebody come and took her to the hospital but they said there was nothing they could do for her and sent her on back home. They knowed all the time she was a gonna die. She was gut-shot and dieing a slow, horrible, painful death. At that time, they didn't have to report it to nobody so they just sent her on back home to pass away.

She was laid out on her bed in agony, just waiting to die. My Dad begged and pleaded with her, promised, swore, he did, if she wouldn't prosecute him and send him to jail, he'd take care of all us kids till we was grown. There was six of us at the time. Had been seven but my older sister Hazel had passed away some time before. I was to little to know what happened to her.

Now we all stood around wide-eyed, quietly, knowing this was bad…very bad..

I remember well that awful time though, how sick Mom was. All us kids was told to go out and play and to stay quiet. My uncles wife stayed with her and sorter watched after us kids.

We'd come in of a night and eat our supper and quietly go to bed. My sister Gertrude was eleven years old, Flora-belle was seven, Frank was nine, Chester was five and Carl was one. I was between Chester and Carl. But we was quite. We played but we never made no noise. You know how it is when something is so bad wrong that you cant even think about it. There's just a bad feeling ever-wheres so we was real quite morning to night. Unnaturally quite for noisy children.

My Mom suffered ten thousand deaths 'fore she finally died. Us children was shipped off to Gran-ma's at Rock Creek, KY soon as it happened. I don't remember any of the funeral. I don't remember to much excepting for being in Gran-ma's care and going home with her. Uncle John had brought her to the funeral. Dad took us all to Gran-ma's soon as the funeral was over and soon as he could get shed of us.

Uncle John heard Dad tell the man that run the country store there to let Gran-ma charge anything she needed to feed us and he'd pay for it. I reckon that's exactly what she did. Gran-ma run up a purty good sized bill but Dad never paid a dime on it. I guess the store keeper there knowed Gran-ma and the situation she was in. He was good to let her charge what she needed just on and on.

Gran-ma was good to take us in though, she didn't have to. She wore long dresses and always had an apron on. When she went out in the sun, she wore a black bonnet, that I'm sure she made. She kept needle and thread handy all the time to mend rips and tears. With all us youngens to look out after, there was always a lot of rips and tears.

She was like a lot of the older folks of the time, she cared for our physical needs, seen to it we was fed country vittles and clothed. She made the girls flour sack dresses and underwear when she had the empty sacks and the time. We was a heavy burden on her and she worked hard.

She was quiet and soft spoken but she expected us to mind her without question, which we mostly did. She could be sharp with her words and the peach tree limb was always handy to tan our hides when we done something wrong. She never hugged or told us she loved us. I guess like a lot of folks of that time, she thought we ort to know she did 'cause she did take us all in.

How well I remember playing in the Rock Creek graveyard. We'd play hide and seek behind the trees and marker rocks. We was just kids. Kids are kids no matter what. We come in home 'fore dusky dark, in time for supper. Gran-ma always had supper ready. Pinto beans and corn bread and fried 'taters one meal, fried 'taters and corn bread and pinto beans the next.

Another thing I do remember while me and my brothers and sisters lived there at Gran-mas. I was still in diapers and I took a notion to look down into a bee-hive. I went and took the top off. I slipped the rock off the top and then the loose boards. Them bees come a swarming out and simply covered me up alive, stinging me ever-where. I run to the house hard as I could go, screaming, squalling bloody murder.

Gran-ma was bent over the wash board, hand washing out our clothes and she grabbed me up and rammed me in the tub of water. The cool, soapy water felt good to my burning hide. Drounded a lot of them bees, I 'spect. Good enough for them! The dratted things. Gran-ma picked bee stingers out for the longest time as I wallered around in her wash water. I was in pure pain misery. I screamed and squalled at the top of my lungs. I seen sympathy in my Gran-mas eyes that day.

I remember well how I swelled up and them burning bee stings. Why, I swelled up twice as big as I was supposed to be. I guess Gran-ma doctored me good for as you can see, I survived that, though I don't know how. A body gets that many bee stings is as good as dead. Gran-ma must of had some real good medicines she made out of herbs. She kept me slathered down with something or another ever little bit. I didn't like the smell of it, stunk like quarn, but it helped the burning and itching so I accepted it readily. Actually, it felt purty good on my lumpy hide.

I wasn't allergic to absolutely nothing after that. All them stings done something to my constitution, I guess I was filled so full of bee venom and survived it is why. Wasn't a bit of fun at the time but served me well over the years. I didn't have to watch out for poisen ivy or nothing like that.

Another thing that I remember well that happened while we were there. The store Gran-ma bought groceries at got jelly in five pound wooden buckets. They'd cut you a chunk of jelly out of the bucket and wrap it up in wrapping paper and sell it to you that way.

Well, one day, that store give Gran-ma this here wooden bucket that was supposed to be sold out empty. They usually scraped it out down to the last drop but this'n had a little left pink scrapeings left in it. Me and my brother, Chester, we scraped the sweetening out of the bottom of it and eat it. It tasted real bitter sweet and we eat what little they was, graveling it out with our grubby fingers.

Well, Chester took ptomaine poisoning and died. He was just little, about five years old at the time. I don't know how come I managed to survive. All them bee stings, maybe? I didn't even get sick.

I don't know how but uncle John found out Dad hadn't paid a thing on our feed bill at that grocery store. He come in his A-model Ford and got us, gathered up what few belongings we had and brought us in to what used to be home, to Wallings Creek, KY, the house where my mother was shot in.

I guess it was a big relief on Gran-ma to be shed of all us youngens. But we seen her standing out in the yard a shading her eyes and a looking after the car 'til we went plumb out of sight. I imagine she was wondering what laid in store for us when we got to where we was going.

I think she sorter hated to see us go, her being alone and all. I looked back long as I could see her. We didn't know what lay in store for us either. I guess if we had, we would have begged to stay with Gran-ma. Uncle John didn't give us no choice, though.

Uncle John was awful upset when he got us home and snapped at Dad, " They're your kids, now you take care of them!"

Meantime Dad, (the old man) had re-married. I don't reckon Mom was much as cold in her grave 'fore he got re-married. He never did get punished for what he did to Mom, neither. He slick dab got away with it. His new woman had three kids of her own. She didn't even know 'the old man' had all of us for he never even mentioned us at all till after they had been married a good while. Her oldest boy was two years older than me and then she had another younger boy and a girl.

His woman was as purty a woman as they ever was and 'the old man' was absolutely crazy about her. Boy, she was real mad when we got there cause when he did tell her about us, he had promised her that Gran-ma was a gonna raise us all till we was grown and take care of everything.

Man! Was she all shook up when we showed up. There was five of us and with her three, that made eight. She had a belly bulge, too, so her and him was expecting a little one, together, looked like. Him and her went on to have six or eight more youngens over the years.

She hated it so bad that we was there that she developed a mean streak in her and made it rough as possible on us outsiders. Things was purty bad. She cooked for 'the old man' and her youngens and they eat good but she never would call us five outsiders in to eat. We done without, lesson we just happened to go in when something was ready. Then she grudgeingly allotted us out a little.

We could all tell she didn't want to and begrudged ever bite we eat. All of us got purty skinny, mostly bones and stringy muscles with skin stretched over them. That woman didn't care. Never bothered her or her youngens a bit.

I figured out a way around that though. I crawled in under the floor ever day and listened till I heard pots and pans a rattling, then I'd come out of my hiding place and show up at the table. She couldn't hardly avoid giving me a little something or another to eat. I tell you, it was every man (or boy or girl) for hisself around here. We learned purty quick that we had to take care of ourselves. She sure wasn't going to.

Well, we moved from Wallings Creek to Allias, KY when I was about six years old. I started to school in first grade there. I had a kidney problem, had it for a long time, I just dripped all the time. Didn't drink enough water, for sure. Guess I kept an infection all the time. Couldn't help it, couldn't do a thing about it. Little boy, you know, I didn't know what to do about it 'cept just let it drip.

I just had me one outfit of clothes, one faded pair of over-halls and a thin shirt. I wore them all the time. I slept in them, wore them to school and I stunk like a dad-gone pole-cat. Life was miserable as heck. I can't recollect much about my brothers and sisters at the time, I was so miserable myself.

Things was rough as a cob for me. I guess it was for them, too. I know none of us got treated like the womans children. They eat good and had decent clothes and fairly good shoes to wear.

I slept in a cold room of a night, didn't have no covers and I'd just about freeze to death. 'Course, my britches and straw-tick mattress bed was wet and cold, nearly froze stiff. Rest of us slept in there, too. They didn't have no covers neither. Nobody wanted to sleep with me on account of the wet, stinking bed but they had to.

I had a pair of shoes but they had holes in the bottoms. In the wintertime, they'd get plumb full of snow. Didn't have no socks.

When I out-growed them, I had to wear them anyhow. Wasn't no more to take their place. They rubbed the ends of my toes raw. When they got so bad, they had to be passed on down to the next one they'd fit.

Like I told you, now, some of my situation was purty sad. This is one of the sad parts. I mentioned rediculous, it was both sad and rediculous. Unless you was there and lived through it, you can't hardly imagine it really happening, but it did. But, oh, yes, it did. Remember, this was in the late twenties, early thirties. Things wasn't nigh as structured back then.

I didn't go to school much, a day or two ever now and then. When I did go, I got up and left the school room if I took a notion to. Don't have to even tell you that I didn't learn much a-tall, never got much of a education. I had about a mile to walk to school and when I got there, teacher always set me by the radiater, school had radiater heat, to thaw me out, I'd be so froze.

Soon as I started thawing out and warming up, I'd start in a stinking and I'd have to leave the durn room. I could leave anytime I wanted to anyhow. But it galled the fire out of me to have to leave on account of that. I'd stay an hour or two or whatever I wanted to or could get by with, get warmed up, then get up and leave. Ever-body moved away from me and was just glad to get shed of me, I guess.

Ah, I had a heck-of-a-time, I did.

Them kids around there made all manners of fun of me, too. (sigh) A lot of the time, they'd get away from me where I couldn't hear exactly what they was a saying but I could see them whispering and pointing and sniggering at me. I knowed it was me they was making fun of.

But they stayed a good arms lengths away, never got right in front of me or up in my face. They knowed if I ever got a holt of them, I'd beat the crap out of them. I had a fight about ever day anyhow and I shore didn't know when to quit. There was always some old boy that wanted to see if he could get the best of me. Sometimes I'd be beat to within a inch of my life but nobody never knowed it. The other feller was in as bad a shape, or worse, as I was.

You wouldn't think a little kid could get to the point that he just didn't care or that his hide could get so thick and tough. I seen a lot of unusual things happen in my lifetime. Things that most people don't ever see in their whole life. I had to grow a thick hide to survive.

I was strong from all that, in spite of the lack of grub. Knotty as a pine ball, I was, and bristley as a cockle-burr. I guess I'd seen way to much in my few short years. Just living day to day was a struggle. But it was all I knowed to do at the time. You know, a body has to get by and get by, I did.

I guess I was about seven years old when I decided that was........ heck!.....I could do better than that someplace else. Every day when I was out and about, I began to look around to see where'd be the best place for me to go to. Need to just get away from where I was.... existing...couldn't say....living....'cause it shore wasn't much of a life.

Thats when I discovered the company store dumped their garbage in a pile out back of the store. I found out I could go down there and eat my meal from the garbage dump, then I'd go on in home, closely eyeing ever place that could be a possibility for me to move to. I looked at ever cave, ever culvert, ever bridge anywhere close around. I was determined to find some place where I could live and survive.

Then I'd go on in and sleep in my cold bed and get up and do the same thing all over again. I'd eat half rotten potatoes from the dump, all kinds of 'to far gone' fruit. Once in a while, there'd be a bone in there that the dogs hadn't found. You could tell by the smell of it if it was rotten or not. I liked to find them when they'd just been discarded. That way I knowed they was still in purty good shape.

I never eat it if it was to bad stinking. I'd just brush the skippers off, if there was any, (that's them little white worms that got on the fatty salt cured ham and shoulders) when I picked it up and make shore there wasn't any left on it. Didn't much care to eat them things. I wasn't to picky about my grub but there's limits a body will go to. Didn't want me no skippers for dinner or supper neither. I may have eat some of them but if I did, I never knowed about it.

But they surely must have been some nutrition in what I found to eat for I lived and growed, stringy I was, but I growed. I'd bust that bone up with a big rock and build me up a little fire somewheres out of the way. I'd put pieces of that bone in a discarded peach or bean can and cook it done. Sometimes I'd be so hungry I couldn't hardly wait till it got done and I wouldn't. If there was a well cured, hard, lean piece, without any signs of skippers, I eat it raw. It was good.

My thoughts now was, why go home at all? What was the point? I wasn't wanted there. Nobody cared. So I decided today was the day to up and leave and just not go back home. I was seven years old. Shucks, I was peart near grown. I could handle whatever situation that come up. Let the others take care of theirselves, I was a leaving, I'd had it up to the gills.

So that day I left with the clothes on my back, that's all I had anyhow, and just never went back.

I had picked my spot out a while back that I thought was the best place for me to go to. There was a good stand of trees circling around this bridge that would knock the wind off in the winter and provide wood for me, too. I chose that bridge for that seemed the best possibility for my situation.

I fixed me up a place nunder there. Got me a thick cardboard box, made me a little house against the wind and weather. I could build me up a little fire nunder there and stay purty warm. Heck, I stayed…….. lived……..nunder there. I eat ever meal at the dump… eat better'n I did at home since I wasn't never called to the table.. Nobody come a looking for me. I was purty shore they wouldn't.

I guess the 'old man' and his new lady was just glad that there was one less kid, or youngen in the house. I was just as glad they never come to fetch me back. I probably would've told them where they could go if they had but they never. I mean not a living solitary soul ever come to check on me. I guess my brothers and sisters did wonder what went with me. But if their situation was as bad as mine, they had all they could do just staying alive.

I guess if they'd a had the nerve, they'd a done the same thing. I wasn't short on nerve. I was blessed abundantly with nerve. Took a lot to scare me. Heck, after all I'd been through in my short life, I guess I had sorter built a shell, like a tarpan or box turtle, around me. Hard to get through to me. I was in there somewheres, but you never seen me. My eyes concealed anything that give away a weakness in me. I was strong for a little feller and I dont especially mean strong smelling either.

I lived right there at the river so I'd go stand in the river with my clothes on in the summer time and I kept myself in better shape than I did when I was staying home. I went on to school when they took up books whenever I took the notion, when I felt like it, and stayed however long I wanted to.

I never got treated no different even though I didn't stink as bad as I used to. I was different from them. I was the odd-ball, the outsider. I guess most all them was poor but I was destitute. One outfit of thin, worn clothes was still all I had in the world. I still slept in them and wore them every day. Most all them youngens had more than just one set of clothes their Mam's had made for them. Didn't nobody there, that I knowed of, have store boughten clothes. My ragged overhalls had seen their better days.

I remember well one incident, coming from school. I always went a different way than the rest of the kids did. They didn't want me walking with them no-how and therefore I stayed away from them. I was a loner and didn't much care if I was. Nobody give a hoot about me anyhow. Nobody.

I'd come around the hillside on this dirt road and had to pass five or six weather boarded houses, grouped together there. I knowed when I was coming close by the smell. There was a homey smell that come from most all the houses. Supper smells and such like. Clothes lines filled with sweet smelling clean clothes flapping in the breeze. Old hounds laying in the yards too lazy to even bark at me.

My belly growled so much that I always hurried on apast them anyhow. Didn't want none of them to think I needed supper or anything of that nature. I'll find me some supper on my own here in a little bit. Kept my head down and trucked on by hard as I could go. I may have been young but I was still proud. I knowed how to take care of my own needs.

Then one day, just ahead of me, there was three purty good sized boys squatted down a playing marbles in the middle of the dirt road. Had their circle scratched out in the road and was taking turns a shooting, flipping them aggies, hopeing to win the other fellers marbles.

I kindly went around them, skirted around to the side a bit and they just stopped playing marbles and stared. They eyed me like a pack of starving wolves looking at a lone chicken.

Which one of them would get me? I got that tight feeling in the pit of my gut. Tensed up and ready. I could smell it. I could tell it was a coming. I watched them out of the corner of my eye. I knowed they was a gonna start a fight with me. I just hoped they wouldn't all pile in on me but I figured they would. That's the way it usually went..

They all jumped up of a sudden and one of them run up and headed me off. No escapeing. They was before me and behind me. That one that headed me off started hitting on me, hard. I was doing ok with him but the other two jumped in and commenced to hitting me, too. I slid out and away from their fists and grasping hands. I could be as slippery as an eel when I needed to be.

When I finally did get free, I took off as fast as I could run. There's a time to stand and fight and a time to get away and right now was the time to get away.

My feet thudded the ground as fast as I could pump my scrawny legs, kicking up dust and gravel, paying no mind what-so-ever to the rocks hurting the bottoms of my feet. I wasn't in to bad a shape but it didn't take long till I was breathing hard.

This great big boy was a running after me. I could hear him a panting as he come up behind me and I knowed with his long legs, he'd be a gaining on me ever step. He had eat since I had, too. I was about ten feet ahead of him but I knowed I had to do something and do it quick. He was a gonna catch me shore and finish the job them smart alecs had started.

As I run, I kept on glancing to the side of the road and ahead of me I spotted me a rock about the size of your two fists. I grabbed it up right quick and just stopped running, come to a screeching halt, I did. I could hear that big boy a coming up behind me and I timed it just right.

I whirled around and struck him with all my might right in the temple. He went down like a pole-axed steer. I thought shore that I'd killed him. Them other boys screeched to a stop and stared with their mouths a hanging open. They looked back and forth from their buddy to me. They didn't want none of that, from this little scrawny boy still holding the rock drawed back at the ready.

It happened right beside some fellers house and he come a running out there. I figured he was one of them boys Pap. I quickly lowered my hand with the rock in it and backed off a ways and stopped. Then I stood and watched the goings ons. I dropped the rock down in the ditch behind me.

That man hurriedly stooped down and looked at the boy a laying sprawled out there with blood seeping out from the ever-growing lump on his temple. Must have been a watching us from somewheres or heard them other fellers a yelling, one.

That man, he run and called an ambulance and they finally come and hauled that boy off to the hospital. I still stood a ways back and watched. I was ready to take flight if anybody took after me but they never. I plodded on around the hill by myself, head down. A body does what a body has to do.

Next time I seen that boy, he had a bandage around his head and they had brung him out to lay on the front porch in the sun. He never bothered me no more after that. Nor none of the other bunch there did, for that matter.

I got through third grade, going once in a while when I took the notion and then I just plumb quit. Nobody never said nothing about it, nobody seemed to give a dad-gone where I did or didn't. Nobody never even come to check on me even then or nothing when I quit going.

The bridge was a good roof over my cardboard home and I stayed nunder the bridge of a night, wandered around of a day, here yonder and about.

But I had to fight all the dad-burn time, somebody or another jumping on me just for the heck of it. I guess I had a reputation for fighting at the drop of a hat and sometimes I guess I'd drop it myself. In the long run, though, it paid off for me, I was able to protect myself.

I learned how to do a lot of little tricks and take care of situations as they come up. That helped me out a whole lot when I went into the Army. Course that's a ways on down the road from here.

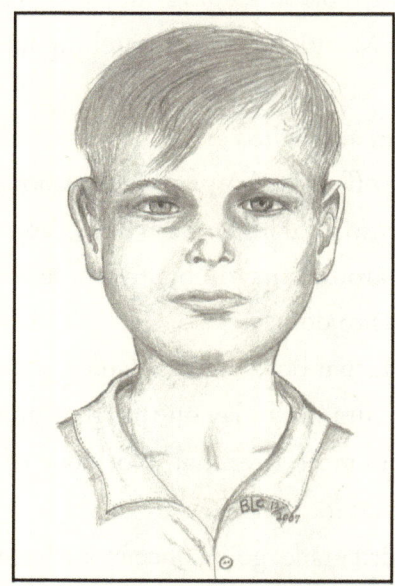

Chapter 2

Rock Throwing

I startled awake and jumped up awful quick out of my cardboard house nunder the bridge. Cracked my head on the bridge supports, I jumped so high. Do that a lot. Seems to me like I'd learn but it looks like I never do. I eased back down inside my box slowly on my bed of dry leaves and rags, rubbing my head. Almost got a crick in my neck, too, from a laying quiled up there. Necks sore and stiff. I'll have another lump on my head, too, you betcha.

Old heads as knotty as a tom cats anyhow from all the fighting I have to do. Hair sticks up ever-which-a-way where I lay on it and it never gets combed, and if it comes right down to it, washed and combed. I don't wash it in the wintertime. Only time it gets washed in the summer is when I dive in and play around in the river.

Same old dream though, and when the gun blasted, I jumped, just like I did that day a little over four years ago. I have this same dream often, not ever night but often. I don't guess you could call it a dream since I lived through it when I was three and a half years old but I don't know why I have to live through it over and over again this way. Pure misery it is, to have to relive it this way.

I think maybe if I'd just get up and brush the leaves off me and the cobwebs from my mind, I'd get to feeling better. I rolled over and slid out from my cardboard box and stood up. Little fire in the center of my box was long since burned out, a few ashes and burnt charcoal ends of sticks left to show there had been one.

And of course, a greasy spot where I done some of my spit cooking. (That's where you take whatever meat you have and put it on a stick and roast it over the fire) Sometimes there's enough fat and lean meat on one of the bones I find to roast over my little fire.

I done that outside my box in good weather most always and whenever I could. Kept matches in my over-hall bib pocket that I'd bummed in a little tin box that I found at the dump. Sealed up real tight. That kept them dry. I guarded them close. Meant the difference in cooked and raw, whatever I eat.

I stretched my arms overhead and nearly ever bone in my back and neck cracked and popped. Felt good. I took a deep breath of the dewy, sweet smelling air, pine and cedar, lingering wood smoke and warm dry leaves. A body could breathe all the way to the tips of their toes in this clean air.

Free as a bird, I am, ain't nothing like it. Ain't nothing like refreshing morning air, neither, sun peeping over the top of the mountain, nigh good as a cool drink of water. I am feeling rough and tough this morning and can take care of what ever I need. But I'm a little hungry as always. Belly's used to that. But I did okay.

Nature calls and I take care of that business in the trees. Nobody to see me down here no-how. Fact is, I don't see to many people around here. I don't bother nobody and nobody bothers me. Only thing I have to worry about is the wild animals and painters (panthers) and I don't even see to many of them.

I hear them coming around of a night sometimes a scratching around but I aint scared. They wont bother me none if I don't bother them and I sure as heck aint a gonna bother them. Truth be told, I'd ruther face a mountain wild cat than some people I know. I usually just prop my cardboard door shut and lay real still. Aint long till they go on their way when they find I aint left out no scraps. I aint got scraps to spare since thats what I eat. I don't discard much of nothing.

Sometimes I lay outside my shelter on the big flat rock by the river with my arms behind my head and just look at the stars. But I only do that when it's nigh light as day. I aint really scared but I don't want no painters slipping up on me. There's billions of twinkling stars in the clear Kentucky sky and the milky way that almost hurts your heart to look up at them, they're so purty.

Sometimes I fall asleep on warm nights just gazing at the stars. Then it cools off enough to sleep inside, and I usually wake up and crawl into my box shelter. Aint lonesome but a little, never knowed much other way than this. Can't help but wonder, once in a while, how my brothers and sisters are doing. Don't linger on it though, brings back to many memories that I don't want to even think about.

Odd how the rock where I got my box set up gets real warm from the sun in the summer-time. Too bad it can't hold that same heat in the winter time, too. Oh, it does where I have my little fire. That rock stays warm for a while after the fire is long gone out.

More than one time I've went to sleep outside and woke up with rain splattering down on my face. Just a summer shower but I always hurried inside anyhow. I was already wet so I usually started up my little fire and stripped off my over-halls and shirt. Laid'm out before the little fire. They'd be dry 'fore you knowed it. Then I slept sound with the rain softly falling on the trees and the running waters of the river. It was a comforting sound to me. I liked to hear it day or night.

River got up sometimes and got muddy as heck when it rained a lot or when it snowed a lot and then melted. But my box was well above the high water line. I aint worried I'll get flooded out. Stuff washed down it when it raged on, tree limbs and trash, stuff like that.

But it never did get up enough to run me out. One time a big piece of metal, I think it was a car hood, washed down the river but it tumbled and splashed end over end and went right on. I watched it out of sight. Couldn't do a thing about it. I sorter wished it had washed up to where I could have got it. I could have done something with it, for shore. But I was smart enough not to risk my neck over it. Let it go. Another piece will come by here and maybe stop off.

I thought I'd santer on down to the dump and hunt me out some breakfast directly. Luck was with me that day. I found me a big hambone with a great big chunk of lean and fat meat left on it, the lean hid behind the fat. Guess who-ever the cook was thought it was all fat and gristle. But that's usually kept to season beans with. I didn't understand but took the bone gratefully.

It didn't even have nothing but a few coffee grounds on it this morning. It smelled good. I'll wash it in the river extry good and take my forked stick and roast me some over my fire. It'll go down good this morning. I guessed it was meant for me to have.

The fat dripped into the fire and hissed and spit. Good thing the fire is in a crevace, a curved out place, in the rock. It's black greasy looking there from where I've cooked before, but who cares? Not me. And they aint nobody else to care. Smells like home to me.

My hands are chapped rough and dirty looking. I wash them once in a while in the river, I guess is why. My face and ears don't get washed much unlesson I go for a swim in the river. When it's good and warm, and sometimes not so warm, I like to wash off and then play in the shallower water. I like to dive to the bottom and come up with a mouthfull of rocks. It's just a little game I like to play ever so often.

One time I scooped up a fat, live craw-dad with the rocks. It wiggled in my mouth and I let it go a lot faster than I picked it up. Tell the truth, that game wasn't nigh as much fun to play as it was before. I'se always afraid I'd scoop one of them things up. They was good to boil for soup but I liked to catch them with my hands and not in my mouth…and them wiggling and raw.

As I began to grow a little, sometimes I hung anound with some boys that was sorter like myself…didn't have much to do. Didn't like school so they didn't go either. They was scrawny, rough and crusty as I was. I never knowed what their situations was 'cause we never talked much about it.

I expected theirs wasn't to much different from mine except they still went on home of a night and I give that up a long time ago. When we did get together, we whiled away the days…just messing around, walking here yonder and about.

One day a bunch of us boys was a hanging out at a gas station place where they sold gas and they sold beer in there, too. They was a few old ratty tables and a bunch of old guys hung out in there. Three or four of us boys hung around there sometimes. You know how curious boys are, they like to be with grown up men and watch whatever it is they're a doing, see what's a happening. Even me. If I got my druthers, I'd heap druther be with some of the older guys than the ones my own age usually.

The old guy that run the place was purty hateful sometimes. We put up with it to get to hang around there…….till he got down-right mean…..

One day he told this one boy, now he was a purty good sized guy, this old guy nodded his head towards us and said to that husky grinning boy, "See them fellers over there?"

He was a talking about me and them other boys that was hanging out with me. We all eyed him to see what he was a gonna say. It can't be good.

That store keeper smirked a bristly mustached, yellow toothed smile and said, "Throw them fellers out of here and I'll give ye a nickel."

Just wanting to see a good tussle, is what he was up to. Figured he'd see a tussle with at least some of us and that tall, muscular boy. That red-headed, red-faced boy grinned even bigger, from ear to ear. He started eyeing each one of us, picking out who he thought would be easy to toss out.

The store keeper'd point his finger at one of us and that big old boy'd throw him out. Just grab him right up and fling him right out the door, is what he done. Didn't give him much of a chance to defend him-self. They'd dingle in mid-air, their arms swinging round and round, hitting nothing. He'd go and get the next one by the galouses and heave him out the door.

We all wore over-alls, mine was peart nigh up to my shins, (high water britches) and that's what he'd grab, the galouses. Sure didn't seem to be much could be done about it. That'n would go a sprawling out the front door and off the porch, into the dusty road. None of them scrawny boys I hung around with, didn't or couldn't, put up much of a fight.

I was sorter waiting for him though. Life on my own had learned me a lot of hard lessons. I'd already graduated from the University School of Hard Knocks. I knowed he was gonna grab and try to fling me so I seized my body up as tight as I could force it to be. I figured that way I probably would be almighty heavy to fling. I tensed up even more, sort of like a fist.

If you tell somebody to squeeze their fist as hard as they can, then say 'now squeeze it a little harder,' they always can make a little tighter fist. I was tight as I could get. I was next, I was the only one left to fling. The store keeper grinned and pointed his large knuckled finger at me.

Then here that big old boy come over there to where I was a hunkering down and grabbed a holt of my galouses. I felt the galous give and pull loose under his large paws. That tore it! Aint nobody a grabbing a holt of me and flinging me nowheres long as I'm alive. He was a clawing for a holt on my shirt, the other galous or anything. I felt his fingernails dig in as they scraped hide off my chest.

Just as he gathered a good holt on my flimsy shirt, I rammed my head back into his face and hit him with every bit of strength I had, fast as a snake a striking. Smashed his nose all over his face. Blood spewed down over his lips. His eyes widened. He shore wasn't expecting this.

We went to fighting and we tore that place all to smithereens inside, knocked the screen door off and went on outside a fighting. We knocked over displays that store keeper had out front and bashed them to pieces. That feller like to beat me to death but he didn't know anything about it.

He was the first one to quit and it was 'cause he wasn't able to go on anymore. I was beat to a bloody pulp but he quit first. That gent was purty bloody his-self and didn't seem to want no more. Well, I didn't either but I would've kept on a going 'till I was unconscious, I guess, if he hadn't quit.

My over-halls had one galous still hanging on. There was blood all over them, mine and his combined, I was sure. We was both heaving for breath, bent over, our hands on our knees, eyes nearly swole shut, still half-lidded snake-eyeing one another, waiting for a chance to k.o. the othern. When he started in a gagging, I knowed he was done. I'd hit him so many times in the gut with my hard fist,

I guess it made him sick. Durn, I was half sick myself. No way was I gonna gag though. I'd die first.

That store keeper's one eyebrow, all the way across, above his eyes, twitched up and down, his eyes was round as the big aggies, as he stared at both our bruised and bloody car-cuses. His mustache curved downward around his open mouth. I don't think he expected this, since that old boy was so much bigger than me. He didn't act like he did anyhow. He didn't know who he was a dealing with, I guess.

Or, heck, maybe he did, he probably knowed I'd be the one that'd give that big old boy a hard time. Well, he ask for it and he sure had a dang mess to clean up where we had fit and tore things all to pieces. I tied my one galous back together in a knot and crippled away from there spitting blood. My shame faced buddies follered along behind me with their heads down and their faces red.

One defended his-self hotly, " If he wasn't so quick to grab my galous and him so much bigger'n me, I could a got him and got him good!"

The rest just hung their heads and never said much, muttering amongst theirselves. I didn't even bother to listen to'm. All it meant to me, was I could take care of myself. Whooo, that gent was big.

I had a hell-a-of-a-time, fighting around everywhere. I was mostly a loner, tried to stay mostly by myself on that account. Ah, I guess I was kinda hard to get along with…..I guess I was kinda bitter, but then I dont have to tell you that. I 'spect you done had that figured out right from the git-go.

I liked to watch them older guys play what they called Five-up, a card game. They'd gather up and play partners. They'd go down on the railroad tracks to a cut and play Five-up. I really liked to watch them play. I could watch them for hours on end. It was enjoyment to me to watch who lost and who won.

I'd hold little secret bets with myself as to who would win and who would lose and the loser'd get mad. For when they lost, they usually did get mad. I'd edge in real close, as close as they'd let me, so I could see real good. They never seemed to care to much.

One day, there was this one old guy that was losing bad that day, and he decided to take it out on me. Told me if I didn't leave and leave right then, he was a gonna kick my rear end. I didn't even act like I heard him and made no attempt to move. He grabbed me up by the hair of the head and beat me up real good. He did boot me in the butt three or four times. He ort to of knowed better. He soon learned better.

When he finally let me loose, I was in a such a rage I couldn't hardly see straight but I stayed real cool on the outside. I just calmly walked away and down the railroad track to where I could get up above them there. I had to walk about a half a mile to where I could come up in above them. So when I got out of sight I hurried along. There was a cliff right above them that was purty much straight up and down. I climbed up the hill to the very top.

I quickly piled me up about a bushel of rocks and sighted down at them men a squatting down in a circle there. Then I started peppering them rocks down at'em. Fast as I let one fly, I snatched up another and let it fly. They separated out quick as a wink and I picked that old boy out of the group. I was so mad that I was trying my dead level best to kill him with them rocks about the size of your two fists.

Dad-gone it! He got away. I didn't know if I bruised him up much or not. I shore as heck hoped so. I was bruised purty much all over, most especially my ego. Took me a long time to cool off. But flinging the rocks with all the strength I had, had took some of the edge off.

Two or three days later, I was standing around not doing nothing and that old gent comes up and grabs me from behind. Held me in a one armed clinch and beat the hell out of me again. He pounded me purty much all over. He hit and hit till he got tired of hitting and then finally he let me go.

I fell forward and he left out of there. Shucks, he'd weigh two hundred pounds, I guess I'd weigh maybe eighty. I was bruised and bloody from one end to the other.

Next morning after he done that, he started down the road to go to work on the tipple, Well, I knowed where he lived and what time he went to work. I was sore as a boil but I got in above him like I did at the cliff place, and piled me up a bunch of rocks, real early. Stuck my pockets plumb full, too. He wasn't expecting it and, MAN! I got him good that time.

Dang! I hit him good a half a dozen times, big rocks, 'fore he ever much as knowed what was going on! Drawed blood, I did, most hits. That showed that old buzzard who he was a messing with. I had filled my shirt-tail full of big rocks, too, so as to have plenty of ammunition in case I had to run. Purty much knowed I would..

He'd try to run me down and I'd pepper more rocks at him and hit him, him a trying to run after me and shield his face at the same time. Dang! He'd stop and I'd take off again, get far off from him, wait till he got in range and hit him again with them big rocks untill he stopped. Then I'd run off to where he couldn't find me. Most times I left him purty dad-gone bloody.

Ah! But he would catch me out somewheres and beat me up again and I'd be the bloody one. That went on....shucks fire..... it went on a LONG time and ever time he beat me up, I'd pepper more rocks at him, two or three times. At first, I just rocked him once but then that got to where once wasn't enough. I was so mad, I'd learn that old codger just who it was he was a dealing with. I'd rock him three or four times for good measure 'fore he caught me once again. Beat me up again.

Finally one fine day, he grabbed me up again. I hunkered down, ready for him to beat the heck out of me. I just knowed....here it come......I covered my face and head with my hands.....

But he hauled me up to his cut and bruised face and looked me right smack dab in the eye and says, "Boy, let's call a truce!"

One of his eyes was black and peart near swelled shut. The rest of his face was no pretty sight either. His whole face was red as a pickled beet.

I nodded slowly and said, "Okay."

It WAS okay with me. Either way. But I was tired of dodgeing him and still getting caught and whupped. I wasn't so mad now anyhow since I felt like I had got the best of him. Me and that old boy got along just fine after that. I'd go on down there and hunker down with them and watch them play cards. They never let me play, I didn't want to nohow. I didn't have no cash money.

Ever now and then though, one of them would send me to the store after something for them, and they'd give me a nickel or a couple of pennies or something. I was pleased to get it. A nickel, or even a penny, bought a lot in them hard times.

I just wandered around of a day here and there when I wasn't watching them men play cards. I had to gather my eats ever day, too. Wasn't much of a problem in the summer, what with the store's dump, and all. Summers was good. I fooled around days on end, wasted time, winter and summer untill I was about eleven years old.

Winters was harder but I survived. That's what it was about... surviving. Along and along, I combed the dump for useable items. Even in that day and time, some things was tossed away that I could use. To the people that tossed them, the items was wore plumb out and no earthly good, but to me they was in good shape. Good stuff I could use.

I found me a coat one day that was well patched and ragged, one sleeve ripped almost half-way into at the shoulder but it was toasty warm. I found me a rusty safety pin and pinned it together good. I was proud to find it, proud to wear it in the winter. Kept me warm, it did.

I found rags that could be used as covers against the blistering cold winter nights. I usually went barefoot in summer but I could usually always find some mens brogans in the dump that I could wear in the winter. Who cared if they was so big that they flopped around on my feet.

At least I wasn't walking flat barefoot in the snow although sometimes the shoes had the soles wore plumb out. Then I had to stick thick cardboard lining in them to keep my feet off the snow. Had to change it most as often as a babys diaper cause that cardboard didn't stay dry long.

I found small boards and odd shaped tin pieces that I could put on the top of my box home for a make-shift roof. I even found a little piece that was perfect for a porch that I propped up with two stacks of pillars of rocks. I laid two big rocks on the top of it, too, to keep the wind from blowing it away. In under the bridge, the snow didn't affect my box to much. But the wind sure did, even with the trees around. Course, they didn't have no leaves on them, they was just bare trees and the fallen dead limbs afforded me wood to burn.

I had to replace my card board box home ever so often. I always lined it with sage grass around the walls for insulation and with leaves covered with rags to sleep on, keeping the center in the middle of it cut out for a little fire to stay warm by. I was ever so careful about my fire. My boxes never did catch on fire but they did get sorter brittle and smoked up.

I left a little hole open in one corner of the top for the smoke to go out. But I was purty well smoked up myself from where I tried to keep my self warm. I mostly stayed huddled up by a little fire in the winter. I hunted up firewood and kept a purty good sized pile just outside my door at all times. You never knowed when a big snow storm would sweep through. I got outside to hunt for grub and when nature called and that was about it.

I never cried. That is, unless you counted the times I got so ferociously mad that tears formed in the corners of my eyes. Once in a great while that happened when somebody got the notion to beat me up. But what was the use in feeling sorry for yer-self? Nobody cared.

And all the crying in the world wouldn't make a single soul care one whit for me. Every tear thats ever been cried wouldn't make no difference to me anyhow. I was used to it. I tried to not ever think about it. One day at a time, that's all we got anyhow, aint it? Yeah. That's all we got. I learned to live one minute at a time...not even one day but one minute....for you never knowed....

Ever day...same as the day before. Take care of necessities.....try and stay warm....search the dump for grub.....catch craw-dads and minnows.......stay out of peoples way....

Then one day, I had an idea when I was about eleven years old. It came to me like a flash of light. I decided there had to be something better than this hand to mouth existance so I decided it was time to leave out of there. I never so much as looked back.

I left my safe place under the bridge and walked away. Soon the invironment would take over where I had been and there wouldn't be no trace of me anywhere. A little greasy spot on the rock, that's all.

Nobody give a crap whether I lived or died anyhow so I hitched a ride on up to Hazard, KY and crawled on a freight train. I thought to myself, 'there's a lot of different places to see and I want to see them all.'

When I left out of there, I didn't know where that train I hopped on was a going, didn't much care. I looked with wide-eyed wonder at the new places I saw and all the people. Lots of different kinds of people. People of all races hoboed. I thought I had a brand new idea. I guess I thought I invented hoboing but I learned fast that I shore never.

I hoboed around from the time I was eleven till I was sixteen years old. Time passed and I usually never even knew what day it was. Ever so often I'd go into a country store and ask what day it was. Sometimes it'd be a month or two a past my birthday. I never even knew when it was or one day from the next. Didn't much matter no how.

I just hopped whatever train that was going through, lot of times right straight back to the same city or town that I had just been in. I didn't know much about this lifestyle but I soon learned which trains was a going where. And I figured out where I needed to go, where the eats was better, which men to hang around with and which ones not to. I'd ease in and eat from a common pot of stew some of the old men at the train yards was a cooking. They'd be gathered up in a patch of trees purty close to the tracks.

One early summer night, stars twinkling overhead, when I hadn't been hoboing around long, I come upon a bunch of old men that had a fire built in a metal barrell and was cooking a big batch of hobo stew. I heard one of them say they had put it on to cook early in the day and it had simmered all day. I never ask what was in it or where they got the grub. You just didn't do that. Wouldn't have been good manners. I just hoped to be invited to eat.

The smell of the stew was tantalizing. Must have been a purty good hambone one of them had found to go along with the vegetables. One old boy was stirring the stew and ladeling it out in tin plates to the men who'd lined up there. He noticed me a standing there in the dark shadows and offered me a tin plate ladeled high with the good smelling stew. I reached out and took it.

I began to eat for I shore was hungry. Something kept on popping and crunching in my mouth, about every other bite. Tasted purty good though. I didn't want to be rude so I chawed and swallered the food without any comment. Sometimes it scratched my throat as it went down 'cause I was so hungry that I wasn't taking time to chew it up real good.

One old bearded guy without a tooth in his head complained, " Dad-blame it, Fred, wha'didya make this stew out of anyhow? What is that in there, that I cant hardly chew up?"

I guess it was Fred that growled, "Quit yer complaining and eat."

We eat and refilled our tin plates. Everybody chomped and eat, same as I did. I listened to the old men talk till late in the night then I slipped out and slept off to the side, out of the way. When I got up early the next morning, I sneaked over and looked in the stew pot. What stew that was left, had several big, fat, cooked up, green June bugs in it. I guessed they had flew in as the stew bubbled and boiled all day.

Well, I was no worse the wear for it, it didn't make me sick, but I didn't think I wanted none of it for breakfast so I lit a shuck out of there 'fore them men could offer me any more. I had had my protein for supper. Didn't want no more.

A lot of interesting things happened during that time. I was in sixteen states 'fore I turned sixteen years old, just a hoboing around from the South to the North to the East to the West.

Chapter 3

Jail Time

One time when I was about twelve years old, I was walking along somewheres in West Virginia, and run into this old boy. He was actually thumbing a ride, hitch-hiking, and he was probably twenty one or two years old. I could tell he was a bad guy, real mean. Untelling what kind of trouble he was in or running from.

I was ready for some company, any kind of company, I didn't care how mean he was, long as he didn't cut my throat in my sleep so he and I walked along together 'till we come to a railroad track. I hadn't spoke to a human being for a long while. My voice was rusty as we made our introductions.

I croaked, " Howdy, there, my name is Yancey. What's your'n?"

I figured he wouldn't tell me his real name as he said, " You can call me Sticks."

What kind of a name is that? But I met a lot of different kinds of characters with all kinds of different names on my journeys so I didn't sweat it. I don't care what he's called. I probably aint gonna call him by no name nohow.

He stopped, set his hands on his hips and looked down the tracks and declared, " If they's a track, then theys got to be a train that'll be a comeing along, and if a train comes along, boy, we'll hop it!"

So he took off down the tracks. Didn't look to see if I was a follering him or not, didn't care, I don't expect. He had already told me he was going to a certain place when we made our introductions. But I follered along, I didn't care where I was going.

We never talked to each other no more but I heard him mutter to his-self something once in a while. I wasn't curious enough to listen to what he was a saying. I could get away from this yahoo any time I wanted to. We walked three or four miles, him a hurrying along in front and me trailing along behind, and come to a station. There used to be stations along the tracks where they dumped off freight and things like that. There was a railroad man standing there with a shopping bag in his hand.

That boy ask him out-right, "Is they gonna be a train through here anytime soon?"

He looked at me and then at the feller I was with, lifted his eyebrows and answered, "I'm a waiting on one now but engine and caboose is all they is gonna be so youse just cant ride it, that's all."

That station was on a curve so me and that bad boy walked around the curve and set down there and waited. We heard the train whistle blow as it come up the track. It pulled up and stopped and quick as it did, we run and got on the cow catcher.

Now the cowcatcher was a contraption they had on the front of the steam engine. I don't know if they have them now or not but back then, they did, the steam engines had a cowcatcher. I guess they was to keep cows off the front of the train. I took it that was what they was for. Me and that boy I was with got on that thing and that train pulled out. Man, he was just a flying, and that was cause he was only pulling the caboose.

He run through a big pasture field of cattle. There was a whole bunch of cows grazing along the railroad track. One was standing right beside the track and time we got to her, the durn cow jumped the track. I just knowed she was a gonna hit me smack dab in the face but she whizzed right on by and somehow missed me, she made it.

You talk about the cow that jumped over the moon. You didn't see this one. Yep, that cowcatcher was to keep cows off the front of the train, all-right. She skimmed over part of it and just kept right on a going. She was still on four legs and she was flat out flying across that field. I don't think she knowed what hit her. I hoped she wasn't killed and just didn't know it.

This guy stopped the train right off, oh, he knowed we was on there all right, so he plumb stopped the train. I guess he wanted to see if either one of us had got killed. This boy I was with, he took off like a scalded dog across the field, other direction than the way the cow took. A few of the other cows scattered and give him room to pass through. Most of the other cows picked the dried grass and eat like nothing had happened. One looked up lazily and gave a long, loud moo. Some had laid down and chewed their cud. You could tell they was REAL bothered by all this. Ha!

Heck, I run about ten feet and stopped, eyeing the engine of the train.

One of them men in the train climbed out and down, I don't know if it was the engineer, brakeman or fireman but he says, " Hey, boy, com'mere! I want to talk to you."

I knowed I couldn't outrun him so I eased on down there and stayed arms length from him.

He said, " Why don't ye get on up here and ride with me? I'll take ye into the yard down there and ye can get ye another train out. Thats as fur as we'll be a going."

I figured he couldn't do all that much to me so I went ahead and got up there with him. No, all he did was, he give me some of his lunch. Turned out, he was a good old guy. That old boy I was with sure missed out. I don't know what ever happened to him, I never saw him no more on all my journeying. When we pulled into the railroad yard, there was a pick-up truck parked there.

That railroad man said, " Ye see that truck a setting over yonder? Go over there and that feller will see to it that ye get something else to eat and he'll find ye a place to sleep tonight."

I said, " Fine, alright, I'll do that. And I thank ye for the dinner and for letting me ride in the cab with ye."

I went on over there and the man leaned over in the truck seat and opened the passenger door. I crawled up in the pick-up. That man in the train must have got a hold of him through radio or something 'cause that man in the truck took me over to a restaurant. Wasn't nobody in there except the waitress behind the counter and he went over and talked to her.

She looked at me intently as he talked, then she come over there and got me and took me to the kitchen part of the restaurant. She give me a pan of water and a rag to wash up with. I washed up good, anyhow cleaned myself up good as I could. Grime in my hands just plain wouldn't wash out.

That girl fixed me up something to eat. I scarfed it down like I hadn't eat in a day or two. I had helped eat the mans dinner on the train. A body in my situation had to fill up ever when they could.

That man was still waiting on me and when I had got done eating, he took me back out to the truck and put me back in it.

He took me up to a jail and said, "Now you listen here, young man, you'll just have to stay tonight, they'll let ye out of here tomorrow."

I didn't care 'cause it was cold weather and I was glad to get to stay there. Actually, I preferred to stay there. He turned me over to this other guy and they got off together a talking low to each other. The other man opened up a cell there and put me in.

Now there was a hallway before you go into the main jail. There was a walkway all around a bunch of cages, and right next to the door, there was a lever.

The man said, "Boy, don't pull this lever now, them guys'll try to get ye to but don't do it 'cause it opens up all them cages."

I was to where I could but I said, "I wont."

I got to walking around there and…heck…they wasn't no place to sleep where I was at and it was cold as heck in there. Only place to sleep was in one of them other cells and only way to get in the cells was to pull the durn lever.

Some old guy watched me eye the lever and he says to me, says in a low, hoarse whisper, "Hey, you, boy, pull that lever and I'll give ye my bunk here."

Wasn't nothing but a steel slab that ye laid on but he had some blankets. Course them guys that was in jail there, they'd done give them some blankets. They laid on one and had one to go over them so yeah, I pulled the lever. The old guy grinned a tobacco stained smile. None of them men didn't get away, though, and I had covers. What good it done them, I don't know.

I got raised all kinds of hell with the next morning but I got away with it. I heard them a talking, in the office of the jail, I was up close with just a door between it and the walkway. Sometimes they left that door open and you could hear them real good.

Every time they changed shifts I heard them say, "Have ye heard from that bad boys daddy yet?"

Other one would say, "Nope, shore aint."

I had give them 'the old mans' address. They kept me thirty days or a little longer. Finally, one day, that same old guy that took me up there come and they let me go with him. He took me out and put me in the same truck. He took me right back down to that same old place where he picked me up.

There was a train that was a making up a load and that feller said to me, "When he gets that load all situated, all built up and ready, they'll be a pulling out of here and you can just go around and get on it and take off, if thats what you want to do."

I walked over there, just fooling around and that old guy set in his truck and watched me. Them men hooked onto a box car, put it right next to the engine. I was gonna get in it later on 'fore it left out but it had one of them little old safeguards on it, wasn't a lock but it clipped together and it was just as good as a lock. It was a little old metal thing and if ye hear this tale, you can figure it out. You know it was put on there to keep people like me out of there.

Anyhow, I slouched over there and leaned up against that box car. I stuck my arm behind me and commenced to bending and bending that thing back and forth till it broke. I knowed I couldn't get in that box car right now cause they was watching me like a hawk. I waited till that train got to going a little, made the first stop, then I hurried over there and opened that dad-burn box car up and got in there. It was full of crates of Maytag washers and things like that.

It was cold weather and you'd just freeze the dickens out of yourself riding on top of a pile of coal. When that train pulled into the next yard, they found out about that box car a being open. They noticed it was open. So they come and rousted me from a sound sleep out of there.

They took me back to jail again. They didn't keep me long though, just overnight, then they let me out. I never done nothing but break that little safe guard anyhow. All I done was that and they decided they wasn't a gonna prosecute the situation, wasn't gonna push it, so they let me go.

Well, I got on a coal train out of there, everything was loaded, they didn't have NO empties. If I went on it, I had to get on top of the coal. You got the dickens froze out of yourself up on top of that dad-burn coal pile with the wind a hitting ye and it down to twenty degrees above zero. I got to freezing so bad that I throwed some of that coal off and I got me some waste out of the hotbox.

Right over each set of wheels, they got what they call a hot box. They call it waste, it's something like mop material and its got oil in it, it's soaked in oil. So I got me a handful and took it up there with me and built me up a real good fire. I made me a hole there and I had me a purty good warm place down in that hole there. It was cozy for a while.

Soon the fire started in to spreading and that coal was a catching afire all around. I just hunkered down and warmed myself by it. Eventually got to be a purty good sized fire and they stopped the durn train. Shucks! They'd seen the smoke!

I looked up and here come two guys from the engine, running around there with shovels. I quit that outfit and lit out for the woods like my coat-tail was on fire, which it wasn't.

Them fellers shoveled all my good, warm fire away and then they went on back to the engine and started going again. I come out of hiding and run alongside and got back in the same dad burn place, done the same dad burn thing. You understand, it was either that or freeze to death.

I done that several times on different trains, and soon as the train stopped, I jumped off and hit the woods. Soon as they shoveled it out and started again, I'd throw some more coal off and make me another hole down in it. It'd be a long time 'fore they noticed it. I got by with it ever time and never did get caught. Maybe they felt sorry for me and didn't try to catch me to much, but I was good at hideing..

Sometimes when that train pulled into the yard, they'd be a heck-of-a-fire. But I had vamoosed long 'fore they ever got back to it. I could make myself scarce right quick.

Chapter 4

Camping by the Creek

Lots of times, I'd call it a day in some old farmers barn. I don't bother nothing but I wasn't above borrowing a little milk from the milk cow while I was there. Usually, old Bossy was in her stall and didn't mind at all if I tossed her a handfull of hay to chew on while I set on the farmers stool and laid my head on the cows warm side. I'd rub my hands a little to warm them and then pull her teats to squirt the warm milk in my cooking can. It usually smelled so good in the barn with the cow munching the sweet smelling hay. I liked the smell of the barns.

I wont take much, don't need much, don't want to take milk that the farmers babies might need. I do wait a while after he's done his milking anyhow of an evening so I don't get much. Just what I need. With a little warm milk in my belly and a nice, big hay loft, I slept like a baby.

My bellies usually purty empty of a morning. Sometimes I don't have any supper except the milk or maybe some berries I pick on the way. In the summer, I picked big juicy black berries. I reckon that's what they are. They are on a thorny briar anyhow and they don't make me sick. I eat a lot of them. Ain't much of a supper but it beat a poke in the eye with a sharp stick. Don't go hungry for long hardly ever.

Ah, I'll pass through somebodys garden 'fore long. There's always something a body can pick and eat. I'm sorter lean and lanky for a growing boy but it don't take much for me to get by.

I can get by on very little, long as I got me some water to drink. 'Course, I've scooped muddy water out of a mules track before when I was real thirsty and swallered it down like it was real good. Well, at the time, it was good, for I was spitting cotton.

I guess I got the wandering fever and I'll just keep a moving on. I don't much care where I am. I haven't got nowheres to go and nowheres to be. Nobody to answer to. Just drifting along.

Sometimes I pass by a house and the old lady of the house feeds me, feeds me good grub, whatever her family is a having for dinner or supper. I don't never have to ask. They just naturally seem to want to take me nunder their wing.

I aint a having none of that. They can feed me and even give me a coat or a pair of over-halls when they notice my wore out ones and I'll take and wear them but I aint staying. No-sir. I know what staying around is like and from what I have experienced, it aint good.

I make no bones about it. I just politely thank them for the good grub and high-tail it out of there fast as I can go. I've seen many a old lady standing at the yard gate with her hands on her hips and a shaking her head as I went on down the road. I tell you, they aint been many places where I was even tempted to stop and stay very long.

I meandered down off a mountain to a gravel road that led to some home-places. I'd been down through here before and I knowed if you traveled several miles to the north, you'd come upon a town. I'd already passed close to it a few days ago, on the outskirts, close enough to check out their dump, and I guess thats about as close as I wanted to be.

I went the opposite direction from the town and soon seen a church house down in the valley with lots of folks a milling around. They had horses or mules hooked to buggys standing around in back of the church. They had saw horse tables set up in front with board tops and flour sack tablecloths with purty patterns sewed together on them. The ladies there was loading them down with all kinds of picnic makings. Delicious smells wafted up the road to me.

My nose told me there was all kinds of fried chicken and chicken and dumplings and a lot of smells that I couldn't identify. My mouth watered and my belly growled so loud that I figured the boys and girls that was playing games in the church yard grass could hear it over the noise of the girls shrieks and the boys coarse shouts.

There was a bunch of men pitching horse shoes in the back of the church yard. They never even give me a second glance as I come closer. The children seen me first and quieted down and stared at me which drawed the attention of the ladies. They all wore long dresses and bonnets and so did the girls.

One of the ladies pushed her bonnet back on her head and spoke cordially, " Well, howdy, there! Wont you jine us fer a bite of dinner adder a while?"

She had a sweating, metal pitcher of some kind of cold drink that fogged up the glasses as she poured and handed out to the children. The children took their glasses and gulped them thirstily. I eyed each glass she handed out. I thought it sorter looked like the lemon-ade my granny used to make. The lady poured a glass-full and offered it to me. I took it gratefully.

Yes, it had delicate slices of lemon in it and I took a small sip. It was wonderful. Just the right sweet, sort of honey flavored, just like my granny's. I closed my eyes that was still crusted over with sleep and drank deep. I was so hungry and thirsty that I slurped.

I downed the whole glass without ever taking it from my lips. It was the best thing I'd tasted since my granny's lemon-ade. I took a deep breath of gratitude and sighed.

The lady looked at me quietly and nodded as she held the pitcher up. I nodded back and held out my glass. She filled it to the brim again. My thirst was somewhat quenched so I sipped this glass slowly to make it last. I looked at my hand holding the glass and noticed both hands was grimy. I wisht I had found some water, a creek or spring or something, to wash up a little in.

But the church folks never seemed to notice how rusty I was or how ragged my clothes was or pretended they didn't anyhow. They just welcomed me in and I know they set out dinner before ten oclock and eat so I could have something in my belly. Or maybe they just got tired of hearing my guts gnaw and growl, I don't know. But I sure tell you this, it was real good grub and I couldn't hold all I wanted to eat.

The ladies bustled around fixing plates for the men and the children. The youngens watched me out the corner of their eyes as I put away the heaping plate-full of home-cooking. It had been a long while.

I got full away to quick and liked to of not been able to polish off that last fried drumstick another lady piled on my plate, along with a big fluffy brown biscuit. I sure did get full way to quick. I guess my bellys shrunk even more than before.

Another one of them women scooped me up a generous piece of four layer dried apple stack cake and flapped it on my plate. It was exceptional moist and sweet with lots of dried apple iceing and just the right amount of cinnamon. I eat it. That buttery cake just melted in your mouth.

I was stuffed so full, my belly stuck way out. Wasn't flat like usual. Sorter miserable, I was, but a good kind of miserable. I sure had busted my hull on the good home made food. I guess they seen that that was about all I could eat. Although they offered more, I quickly shook my head. Didn't want to eat so much I'd get sick right here in front of the ladies and stareing youngens. Now that'd be a bad thing.

That same lady that poured my lemon-ade ask me my name.

She said softly, her voice full of concern, "What's ye name, honey? Aint ye got folks somewheres that be worried sick about ye?"

I shook my head, " Naw, Ma'am, I haint got nobody. I'm on my own but you can call me Yancey, if ye want to."

She seemed to like the name and whenever she talked to me, which was often, she always called me by my name. The youngens gathered 'round and listened to what we both had to say.

She ask me, "Well, Yancey, where is it yere headed?"

She didn't wait for an answer but went on, " Don't ye have somebody, someplace, where ye can go and stay?"

I said, "Naw, Ma'am. I don't have."

She ask more questions. I didn't think she was just being nosy. Here we go again. I can tell by the look on her face, I think she just wanted to take me in under her wing. I answered polite but I never said where I was going or where I'd been. I didn't want no family. I know how families are and how they do one another. Right now, I want no part of one.

She said quietly, shoveing her bonnet back again that had worked it's way down, and raising her eyebrows, "Well, ye know ye'd be welcome to abide with us for a time and a time, more than welcome, now don't ye?"

I nodded, "Yes'um."

But I got up and made ready to leave out even as I spoke. I'm a going. I don't know where, just away from here 'fore I find out things aint as good as they seem.

The lady insisted, "Wait, please."

And she fixed me a big dinner poke when she seen I was fixing to go. Most all the ladies ask me again and again to stay a while and as I shook my head and went to leave, most all of them stood with hands on ample hips, watching me go. And most of them was shaking their heads at one another, trying to figure out why a little feller like me would have the traveling fever. Just couldn't figure me out. Heck, I can't figure myself out so I sure don't expect nobody else to. I just know I gotta go.

The dinner poke was mighty good for a late supper when I got way on down the road. In fact they put in so much grub that I saved some for breakfast. I had plenty of fried chicken for breakfast when I woke up 'fore daylight up in the hayloft in some farmers barn.

Heard some hounds a baying and a bellering across the field. They smelled my breakfast, I guess, for when they was turned loose at daylight, they come and surrounded the barn and barked for a long time. I finally figured out they was three of them. Sounded like a lot more, all the yapping and baying noise they was a making.

I peeped through the cracks in the barn loft and seen a woman at the yard gate a looking towards the barn with her hand shadeing her eyes from the riseing sun. 'Fore long she turned and went across the yard and back into the farmhouse. I just hoped she didn't come over here with a shotgun. Or worse still, her old man.

Her old man did come out to the barn but he wasn't carrying a shot gun, just a plain old milk bucket. I scrooched down in the fartherest corner of the loft so I wouldn't get pitch forked for I knowed he'd probably need to give the cow some hay to milk her. I

knowed there was a cow down there for I seen her last night when
I crawled up in the loft amongst the hay. I just hoped the old man
didn't smell the fried chicken.

Oh, man! I hoped he didn't climb all the way up in the loft! I
held my breath as he swung the barn door open. He kicked at the
dogs as they tried to come in the barn after him.

"What in the world is the matter with ye, have ye lost what little
brains ye have!" He yelled at the dogs. "Aint nothin' here but old
Bossy, shet ye yaps!"

He stepped through and slammed the door after him. The dogs
still cut up some.

The man spoke softly to himself and then to the cow., "Dumb
dogs! Act like they aint got a lick of sense. But you, now, you old girl,
you got all kinds of sense, dontcha, girl?"

I heard him take the pitch fork down off the wall and I knowed
he was going to fork that cow up some hay. He climbed halfway up the
wall ladder and scooped her up a big fork-full, then tossed it down in
the corner of the stall so he could position his milking stool beside her.

He couldn't see me for I was burrowed down so far that
practically the whole loft would have had to have been emptied to see
me. That didn't stop my heart from pounding so hard I was afraid
he'd hear it. But he climbed back down the ladder and I heard him
scoop her out a little sweet feed or corn. She mooed contentedly and
began to munch her feed.

That farmer muttered words I couldn't hear to the cow the whole
time he milked her. She munched her feed and softly mooed once in
a while. Maybe he was a telling her his troubles. Sounded like it. She
sure acted like she understood what he was a saying..

Seemed to me it took him an eternity for him to get the milking
done. Finally the swishing of the milk into the bucket stopped and

he stood and I heard him go out the barn door. He kicked the dogs, yelping, out of the way as they lunged towards the door. He closed and fastened it behind him.

I was glad. I could stick my finger through the crack and turn the button that closed the door when I got a chance to leave out. Who knows if one of them old dogs thought he was a monkey and could climb right up in the hayloft after me? They stayed around the barn all day a sniffing around. I didn't know if they'd leave even at supper time. I was getting mighty thirsty and it was awful hot in the barn.

I stayed right where I was, though. In fact, I waited in the sweet smelling hay till coming dark. But I sure didn't want to be caught in the hayloft again when the old man come to milk tonight. Soon as the hounds had moseyed back across the field for their supper, I high-tailed it.

Didn't throw down the chicken bones. Waited till I got a way on down the road to toss down the picked clean bones. I even sucked the marrow out of the bones, what I could get at and eat the soft gristle off the ends. Some old possum will be glad to find them bones, anyway. Or maybe them old hounds will find them. I wager they do travel this far.

Boy, was I ever thirsty. Wisht I would come upon a good spring. Even a mule track with some muddy water in it would be a welcome sight but it's real dry around here. Don't look like they've had any rain for a while. That's good for my rambling, but not so good as far as thirst is concerned. Ah, rambling aint so bad, nobody to tell you when to rise or when to go to bed, even if ye do get thirsty once in a while.

The dust from the one lane road stirred around my brown, bare feet and settled behind me as I walked. My shoes, such as they was, was tied together and slung across my shoulder, my over-halls was wore slick. I guess it was the dirt and grime that had them slick. I aint seen a creek for a while.

When I do come upon a creek, which I try to foller when ever I can, I wash my britches and shirt out and hang them on the bushes to dry. Don't take them long. I just play in the creek till they get dry. I can swim good which is good 'cause sometimes the creek is purty deep. Or I just get in the water with my clothes on. Either way, they come out smelling a lot better than they did going in.

These clothes is so dirty, it sorter makes me wish I had another pair to change into. Ah, maybe I'll run upon a creek or a rail road track, one, 'fore long. I hope so. I'm so thirsty, even fishy creek water would taste good right now. Or if I could catch a train somewheres, I'd find water at the station. But I always do find water one way or another after a good long dry walk.

Lot of times, I'd start walking down the highway on my hobo trip, trying to catch a ride and I'd walk all day long. Takeing my time, wandering along, looking at birds as they flew and lit. Looking at everything, same only different. I'd be so wore out by the end of the day, I had no trouble sleeping where-ever I laid my head down.

One day I found a dime by the side of the road. Wow! I was really excited. I stopped into a purty good sized grocery store in Appalachie, Virginia and got me a box of crackers. They was a nickel and I could eat off them three days. I opened them 'fore I left the store. Man, was they good!

While I was crunching on the crispy crackers this guy that run the store said, "Where ye hail from, boy? Hey, what's ye name?"

He probably noticed he hadn't seen me around there. Well, I got to talking to the man. But as usual, I didn't give out to much information. Aint nobodys business but mine, is what I think.

I said, after I'd chewed and swallered my bite,"Ah….. I come from here yonder and about. My names Irvin Yancey."

He looked at me slowly and narrowed his eyes at me and said, "Are ye any relation to that Leroy Yancey?"

I put another cracker in my mouth and chewed awhile as I give it some thought then I owned, "Yeah, that's my Daddy."

The man looked off in the distance and said, " He runs a little trade with me here."

I know my eyebrows shot up. Kindly surprised me, it did, 'cause last I knowed of him, he lived in Alias, KY. I tried to digest that fact. I thought to myself, 'well, sir, good luck in getting paid for that'. Ah! The 'old man' probably does take care of the bill here since it's for his second family. I wondered if my brothers and sisters are still with them or if he's got rid of them some way or another.

The grocer nodded up the road and told me, "Leroy Yancey lives up yonder at Dunbar ten or twelve miles from Appalachie."

I couldn't hardly believe it. I thought to myself, heck, I believe I'll just walk on up there. Like to see what's a going on anyhow. 'Bout noon, I took off in that general direction and about seven o'clock that night I walked into Dunbar. I ask around where Leroy Yancey lived and somebody pointed out a white house out to me. I walked on up there, opened the door and walked straight in, a carrying what was left of my box of crackers in the bib of my over-halls.

There was a whole bunch of kids there, actually, what they was a doing, they was having a big party for my step-brother.

I'd come upon a trash dump and found me a purty good pair of shoes in it a while back. They were to big and purty well worn but they wasnt all that bad. Scuffed up and turned up a little on the toes is all. I had put them on my feet 'fore I went into the house.

I was dressed like a vagrant and here they was giving him a fancy birthday party. And I…..eeeeeee…Lord…that messed them up. Everything went quite as a mouse when I walked in there. All them kids in their finery stareing at me with open mouths. I guess they wasn't used to somebody like me showing up and kinfolks to boot.

I said, bold as brass, "Howdy, I'm Irvin Yancey. I'm ye kinfolks!"

Nobody said much of nothing to me and it got mighty uncomfortable after a while. They got to looking at me sorter snooty. That woman was there and she made it plain to me that I wasn't wanted there. I hung around maybe fifteen or twenty minutes and I left out of there. No feller ever felt as out of place in their life as I did. Didn't like the feeling, so I left.

It was worth the ten mile walk…..ah…it was really twenty miles 'cause I had to walk the ten miles back to get to Appalachie to get on the main road leaving out of there. But I didn't do it all that night. I spent the night on the side of the creek.

Caught me some craw-dads and cooked them in a peach can for supper. Had me some more of them saltine crackers. They was broke up but they was good. Slept out under the stars. Laid in the grass with my arms winged back, my fingers laced behind my neck and thought about how surprised they all was. Grinned some to myself. Boy, I was glad to be away from there.

Walked on in to Appalachie in the morning, got me a ride…well, actually, I was plodding along up a long hill and an old truck come along, it was just a puttering and poking along, barely making it up the hill so I run and jumped on the back of it. Rode with that feller to Wise, Virginia.

Went on to many different places, many different towns. Foot loose and fancy free. Went when I wanted to, stopped when I wanted to. Nobody to answer to. Nobody cared enough to look for me. Ah, they probably couldn't have found me even if they had been looking for me (which they wasn't) cause I moved around so much. Wasn't much happening though.

I stayed to myself mostly and just wandered around from place to place, here to there, till I'd find me a place where they was a creek. I'd seine for crawdads. You know, used to be back in them days you could lift up a rock in the creek and they'd be three or four big, fat crawdads nunder it. The creek'd be full of minnows, too. I'd take off my shirt and seine for minnows, too. Shucks, you could eat good off crawdads and minnows.

I'd find me a decent tomater or peach can, one that wasn't rusty, a laying around in the dump somewheres. There was always a dump around close to a town, too. Made a good cook pot to set on the open fire. I'd wash it out some in the creek or clean it out the best way I could.

I'd lay me three or four big flat rocks around the fire. I'd get a good hot fire a going and then I'd set my tin can on the rocks over the fire.

I'd pinch the tails off them crawdads and cook them up. Supper was done and served up in no time flat. Sometimes I'd stay around in that same area for maybe a week or so, just walking up that creek or down it which ever the case might be. Thats where I could find something to eat. I never bothered nobody. Just stayed to myself mostly. It was lonely but I was used to it. Thats all I knew. Sometimes I walked all day long and half the next day 'fore I come upon a settlement or town. Or even a farmhouse out in the country.

I didn't do no talking much so my voice got purty rusty a lot of the time. When I did say something, it come out more as a croak, more like a frog than anything else. It always surprised me when it done that.

In the summer, it wasn't no trouble a-tall to find something to eat. I'd go through somebodys corn field and gather me some roasting ears and throw them in the fire. Time the shuck burnt off them, they was done and they was real good eating. I kept matches to build my fires with, that I still bummed from one place or another. I guarded them closely, too, 'cause they was very important to me. They still meant the difference between eating hot grub and eating it raw. I've eat manys a raw ear of corn or green beans just 'cause I wanted to, though.

I still had the little tin box that I carried them matches in to keep them dry. It was scuffed and worn but it still kept a good, tight seal. I'd done that since I was seven years old. I learned that right real quick. I was careful to only use one match to start my fire.

I'd get me a sharp stick and dig me some 'taters in some farmers 'tater patch somewheres. When I got ready to move on and the grub was a little bit plentiful, I'd take a great big lot with me. I'd unbutton my shirt and cram it with apples, 'taters, roasting ears and such as that.

Them roasting ears was a bit scratchy against my skin but I could bear that. I had to silk them though, 'cause they tickled if I didn't. I'd be swelled up like a big, fat frog in the morning when I set out. But I didn't think that farmer or his wife either one would miss from their big garden patch what little I could carry. And I don't think any of them would begrudge me a bite to eat. They'd probably just think a coon had got in it and carried off some grub.

I never did bother nobody, and only thing I ever did steal was something to eat. Never stole nothing else in my whole life and thats up to today, going on eighty five years old. That's a purty good record. Oh, I had the chance to steal a many of a time and thought about it, I really did, but there was just something in me that wouldn't let me. They was always a way out, other options, in whatever situation I was in.

I figured, now, something to eat….I could get by with that. I didn't figure they'd miss what little I took for I never took that much, you know? Just enough for me to fill up my belly up and get by.

Chapter 5

The Living Doll

In the wintertime, you could usually always find corn a laying around in the fields, that is, most of the time. Sometimes, they'd turn the cattle in the fields after they'd gathered the corn to clean the last of it up. But if they hadn't been no stock in the field, you could find it. I'd shell it off and fill my pockets full, fill my shirt full.

I had a little old knap sack I carried around with me in my pocket, too, and I'd fill that durn thing plumb full and tie it onto my galouses. Then I'd build me up a fire, put the corn in a tin can, set it over the fire and I'd have parched corn to eat. It was real good, roasted that way. The smell of it a roasting was almost mouth-watering. I can almost smell it now as I think about it.

I could eat….I usually always kept something to eat…I got by. There was always something around I could find to eat. Usually, I'd come upon a town or a village, they'd have a dump and I'd first off find out where that was, then I'd go explore it.

Sometimes, I'd find a big old hambone or shoulder bone with a little meat left on it like I used to long, long ago. I'd lay out that old bone and take me a rock and bust it all into creation. Sometimes they'd be some good meat left on it, too. I usually cooked the marrow, too. I could tell if that bone was ruint by the smell of it and if it didn't smell to bad, I'd put it in a can, cook it and eat it.

I kept something most all the time, I didn't go hungry to much. I bummed one meal the whole time I was roaming the whole five years. That time I saw this house and I was real hungry. Hadn't gathered anything up for a while. No corn, no hambones in no dumps, no nothing. I thought 'What the heck!' And I knocked on the door. Some little old gal about my age come to the door.

She was purty as a dad-burn, dark haired doll. I tell you, she was a real knock-out. I tried to say something and nary a word would come past my dry lips, it got lodged somewheres down my throat and stayed there. I tried, I really tried to speak and not one word left my lips.

I couldn't say ONE dad-burn word! My throat and mouth worked as I tried to force them to say something. My mouth was open but my tongue stayed still. That purty little gal got an amused look on her face. Oh, her face never changed expression but her eyes laughed and sparkled with mirth.

My face got red and I got all flustered from not being able to speak. I didn't talk much anyhow because it was usually just me but, yes, I could speak, or croak, if my dad-burn tongue and lips would move ary bit. They seemed to be paralyzed or something, I just knowed they didn't work. I worked my mouth, willing it to speak. Not a dad-burn croak!

So I just give up, and turned around, dropped my head and started to walk off. Heck fire, I was so mad at myself. Heart a pounding in my chest…Dadburn goozle swelled up to where I couldn't speak a dad-burn word. Cat had my tongue or something…. no…tweren't the cat….it was the beautiful girl that had captured it…..with those gorgeous pale blue eyes framed in long black eyelashers….I could feel her stareing at my back intently. But she never spoke a word.

The woman of the house come up and looked out from behind the purty girl as I began plodding off with my red face looking down. My dad-burn belly was a rubbing my dad-burn back bones.

She hollered out at me, "Hey, you, ye wanting somethin' to eat?"

I turned around and looked at her and said, faintly, through parched lips, "Y-Yeah."

Dad-gum, I said something! Ah,…. to the woman though and not to that purty girl. The woman bustled off and disappeared into the house.

I peered around at the girl. She was still standing there. Still as gorgeous as ever.

She looked straight at me and almost straight through me with her pale blue eyes, as she smiled at me and remarked softly, " Hey, what is it do ye want?"

Her voice sounded like water tinkling over the rocks in a clear summer stream. Different. Mesmerizing. My mouth worked a while as I tried to answer her. I swallered hard to wet my throat.

Finally, my throat loosened a little and my lips moved as I stammered out, " Well, c..c..could I have a d..d..drink of water? S… s..shore am thirsty…."

Still couldn't hardly say a dad-burn word…and couldn't talk a-tall without stammering. I never stammered a word before in my entire life. What the….?

That beautiful girl motioned over towards the well and we walked over there to it. My knees was so weak they couldn't hardly carry the weight of my body. She drawed me up a bucket of the coldest water I ever tasted. There was a long handled dipper hanging there and the girl took it up and dipped it in the dripping bucket. She handed it to me and I reached out and took it from her hand.

Her fingers was long, her hand was white, where mine was rusty, sunburnt brown. Then I put the dipper to my parched lips and got me a long, cool drink of that sweet well water. Best stuff I ever tasted.

I couldn't hardly keep my eyes off the girl but when she looked at me and smiled sweetly, I'd drop my eyes. I didn't aim to keep stareing, but I never seen any girl so purty in my whole life. I wondered if she was used to all the boys a stareing at her like this.

She never seemed bothered by it one bit so I guessed she was. Ever time I met her beautiful eyes with mine, she smiled real friendly, her perfect lips curved just right.

I couldn't say diddley squat. I reckon I took my brain out and put it in my pocket somewheres down the road or when I pecked on that front door one.

That older woman, I guess it was the girl's Mam, brought me out half a dozen sand-wiches, bologna and ham. She had me a big old paper sack full of tomaters, cucumbers, and a whole bunch of grub. I finally managed a few words to thank her for her kindness and fled. Couldn't think of no reason to hang around, other than to just stare at that girl and I don't guess that'd do.

Didn't much want to leave, for a while anyway, but I left out 'cause I shore couldn't talk much to that purty gal. She stood out in the yard with her Mam and watched me go. Did she want me to stay? Now that, I'll never know....

I carried that sack of grub around with me till I eat it all up. Just a wandering around, here yonder and about, but I thought of that purty girl often. I often dreamt of what I should have said to her. I wondered if I had camped out there awhile if I could have ever got to where I could have talked to her easy. Ah, just day-dreamed, knowed exactly how I was.

Knowed I most probably never could have but in my day-dreams, we talked easily and often. No stuttering or faltering words....In my day-dreams she liked me.....she liked me a lot.

Everywhere I went, I always found grub to eat, all-be-it sometimes mighty, make do, skimpy. But I always got by. I lived. I survived. I was young, tough and it didn't take much for me to get by. I was wirey from all the walking I done and from all the situations I had experienced so far.

Towards the end of my hoboing around when I was getting on to sixteen years old, I was walking down the street in a town and I passed a whole bunch of houses setting there in a row. There was a guy setting on his front porch. He looked awful familiar to me. I kept on looking at him as I slowly walked.

Finally, I walked over there to where he was and set down on the edge of the porch. He had a piece of cedar wood that he was slowly shaving long sweet smelling curls off of it with a pocket knife. The porch and yard under that sharp knife was already covered with the shaveings. I don't think he was a carveing out nothing, I think he was just a making long curls of the sweet smelling wood, chawing his tobacker and a thinking.

I spoke to him, "Howdy."

He raised shaggy eyebrows and spit off the side of the porch between parted teeth, then answered, "Howdy, do."

He took his time and shaved off another long curl then drawled, "Where ye from, boy?"

I said , "Well, I used to live in Alias, Kentucky. Seen ye setting here and ye shore look awful familiar to me."

He stopped his whittleing and looked me full in the eyes.

He said, " I'm from Alias. I'm just a visiting my daughter what lives up here."

All of a sudden, I told him, " I visited my 'old man' Leroy Yancey, down about Dunbar, Virginia a while back."

He nodded, " Hmmmm, I know yer 'old man' has quit his job down there here not long ago and has moved back to Alias."

Once again, I was surprised. Why I should be, I don't know, but I was. We neither one was to talky but we talked off and on, a few words here and there, for about a half an hour.

He kept on eyeing me, between the long curls of cedar, and finally he asked, "Boy, ye hungry?"

I ducked my head. I was usually always some hungry. I nodded. Then he had one of the kids there to go inside and make me a sand-wich of home made, thick sliced brown loaf bread and salty ham. My mouth salivated at the very smell of it. I set on the porch and eat it while he was talking to me. He talked about 'back home.' I thought it was time to move on 'fore I started thinking about home to much.

I got up and dusted the seat of my britches off, started to leave and he said, "Hey, if ye'll hang around here, I'm a goin' back home tomorrow, and if ye want to go, well, ye can go with me. Stay overnight here, if ye want. Where ye headed anyhow?"

I said, "Heck, I aint got no particular place to go."

We got to talking more and I talked to him for a long time, just plain out told him ever-thing, spilled my guts, I did. After all, he was from home, and I guess that's what made me open up to him. He listened intently to all I had to say, commenting once in a while. I talked till my throat 'bout give out.

I felt better though after we talked, sorter relieved, you know..... like I wasn't plumb alone and had somebody that kindly understood why I was doing what I was doing.

Maybe it was time to go home. I hung around with the old man and stayed the night.

The next day we headed out to Alias, KY. When we got there, I thanked the old gent for the lift. My sister, Gertrude, had got married while I was out hoboing and hitch-hiking around and she took me in when we got there. She trimmed my long, shaggy hair for me like she used to do and I actually felt like I had real family again.

Boy, this was sure different than what I was used to. Gertrude cooked regular meals and fed me good country grub. I set in trying to get a job in the coal mine. I needed the work. I needed clothes and shoes and a good winter coat. I needed some meat on my bones, too, which Gertrude was a trying to fix. Somewhere or another she found me a pair of over-halls that fit me purty good so she could wash what I was wearing. Now I had a pair to wear and a spare. Long and lanky, I was, stringy muscles, no matter what I eat. Hard to gain a pound.

I was a telling my brother-in-law about trying for the job at the mine and he scoffed, "Ah, they wont hire YOU, you're sixteen years old. YOU cant get no job in no mine. You're to young! They aint never a gonna hire YOU!"

I'd show him. I would get the job. I went over to where this feller lived that done the hireing and fireing and waited for him to come out and go to work. I walked with him ever day. Didn't say very much, just let him know I needed a job…just wanted him to know I was available to start to work anytime and could work hard as the next feller. He had about a mile to walk to work and I done that ever morning.

I took to waiting of a evening, too, I'd set around and wait for him to get off from work and then I'd walk home with him. Done that for a while. Finally he said he'd take a chance on it and he give me the JOB! I didn't let on how excited I was.

I just said, " Thank ye kindly."

He knowed about how old I was 'cause he'd knowed me all my life. He knowed approximately my age, anyhow, I got the job and I done alright. I loaded coal in the mine. Hard, back breaking work. They taught me to shoot black powder with a fuse to blast my own holes. It was dark, dirty work but I was just glad to have the job so I worked hard. I'd come in from work as black as coal itself.

You could see my eyes and that's about it. And they was red as fire from being irritated with the coal dust. Now I knowed why the 'old man' was always as black as coal when he come in from work. You couldn't help it. You worked down there, you got covered up with it.

The war was a heating up in Europe at that time. It had begun September the first, nineteen thirty nine when I was seventeen. I was purty much interested in what all was going on. I listened to talk about it ever chance I got. I wanted to know all about it. Very curious. Maybe I'll just go on up there when I turn eighteen and enlist. I'd like to see other places. I'd already seen a lot of the good ol US.

I finally started boarding at a boarding house a lot closer to work after I got the job. This boarding house was close to the river, too, and it had a back porch all the way across the back of it. I bought me a twenty two rifle and I'd set out there of a evening and shoot at bottles and cans and things floating down the river. I got purty good at it. I could hit what ever I aimed at. It was a pass-time for me and I enjoyed it.

I'd come in from the mine, take me a soapy, hot bath and eat supper and practice shooting that twenty two rifle. Since the war was a getting so hot over in Europe, I decided I'd just go ahead and enlist in the Army. Heck, I really did want to see other place 'sides just here. I figured it was time to move on anyhow. So I did. Two years in the coal mine was plenty long enough to hang around in one place, anyhow for now.

I was young. I was eighteen years old, going on forty five…..I'd already lived two or three life-times and was ready to start another one. I sure didn't know what I was getting into though. But I guess if I had known, I'd probably have done the same thing all over again.

Chapter 6

The Army

I enlisted and Uncle Sam seemed awful glad to get me. First time anybody much seemed to want me so bad. The year was nineteen and forty and I weighed in at one hundred and forty pounds. Over six feet tall, I was, and purty dadburn thin. Still seemed like it didn't matter what or how much I eat, I couldn't put on much weight. Still to tough and stringy.

But you know me, I started having trouble right away. They was taking four or five of us over to Fort Thomas, Kentucky, just the other side of Cincinnatti. Just outside of Cincinnatti, we stopped at a little place for a cup of coffee. That guy that took us had stopped there before with men like us so this girl that worked there knew we were fresh recruits joining the Army.

I got to talking to her and she wanted to know if I wanted her to write me and I told her yeah, I did. Course I did. Nobody hadn't ever wanted to write me before, 'specially a nice looking young girl.

She give me her address on a scrap piece of paper and said, "Now, you write me here and give me your address and I'll write ye back for shore."

I went and got in the car and she follered me out and give me her phone number, too. Man! I slid it in my pocket with her address. We pulled out of sight with her still standing there, squinting her eyes in the bright sunlight, watching us go. I felt purty good that she had singled me out to talk to and I hoped she would write to me. That'd be so great.

When we rolled into Fort Thomas, they assigned us a bunk, in among a bunch of them old guys that'd been there a while. Us new'n's was fresh and green as grass. We didn't know much about how things went in the service. But we soon learned. Didn't take us long.

Now they had a day room there that had a phone in it that everybody used so there was a line of men already waiting to use it. There was four or five guys waiting none to patiently for their turn. I guess they all wanted to call their gals or their Pap and Mam one.

So I got in line and waited right along with the rest of them till it come my turn. Finally, I was next in line and the guy that was on it got done talking. He hung it up with his left hand and handed me the receiver with his right hand.

Time I got my hand on it, this big hefty corporal come up and grabbed a holt of the receiver and snapped, " I got to use it, it's an emergency, I'm in charge of these quarters!"

Made me so mad, my temper flared. I'd been standing there for the longest time waiting on the phone and here this yahoo was a taking it away from me.

I snapped, "Well, you can just wait till I use it," and wrenched it out of his hand.

We got into a huge arguement and he give me a shove backward. When he done that, I just jerked that receiver loose from the phone and swopped him over the head with it. He didn't like that a bit. He come at me arms swinging and we fit all over the place. He'd warp me and I'd warp him back and we tore that dad-gone room all into smithereens.

Oh, yes, I got started off on the wrong foot right then and there. I was called in to see the company commander and after I explained the situation to him, why, he never done nothing about it. That corporal guy, if he WAS in charge of quarters, he had a phone in the office he could use. Somebody was a using it, I guess. He just wanted....ahhhh....he didn't want to have to wait and he thought if he throwed his weight around some, he wouldn't have to wait.

He was just unlucky enough to pick me to jump in front of. Maybe some of them other boys might could of been pushed around but not me! I wasn't gonna let nobody bully me around. Never had before, why would I let him now? I was used to taking up for myself...only way I ever knowed how to live.

Well, still, that got me off on the wrong foot. That was even before we was issued uniforms, took two or three days to do that. We was gonna get two sets of fatigue uniforms.

I bought four or five insignas off one of them old guys there. They was little old things that goes on your dress clothes collar, the collar of your coat, they were impressive little signs and I liked them.

I was setting there on my bunk and a sergeant come over to me and said, "You got some insignas?"

I said, "Yeah." And showed them to him.

He said, "Alright, come and go with me."

I follered him into the dayroom. Some guy there had accused me of stealing them.

The Sarge said, "Who'd ye get these from?"

Well, I didn't know the guys name but we walked back in the barracks and I pointed the guy out.

Sarge said to him, "Did you sell this man these things?"

That man said, "Yes, sir, I did."

So we went back in the day room and the company commander was there then. That guy apoligized to me, said, "That other guy said you stole them."

I said, purty perturbed by now," Well, I didn't."

He said, "We know that now…that'll be all …you can go…."

I said, my dander still raised, "Wait a minute, here this guy accuses me of stealing," I growled, "What happens to him? He took it on himself to accuse me of stealing and I never stole nothing in my whole life!"

I excluded the grub I'd taken over the years…That was live or starve to death situation and I never took nothing else that didn't belong to me…EVER…… I'm NOT a thief! Never have been…hope to never have to be.

The man said, "Well, dont worry about it, we'll take care of that."

I told him as I went out the door, my brow furrowed, my fists balled up, "Don't you worry about this situation, I'll handle it myself."

I'd had to handle stuff like this ever since I could remember. And I could handle it now.

That big old sergeant, well, he follered me. We went back in there and that old lying guy was a standing next to his bunk. I was ready for him.

I started to go after him and that old Sarge laid his big calming hand on my shoulder and said, "Don't do that, son. You'll get ye-self in a load of trouble."

So I let it go. I had a reputation, you know, I'd just fight at the drop of a hat and sometimes I'd drop it myself. I finally figured out, you just don't do that. Took a while though. I got into scrapes several times 'fore I caught on. Them guys in the service with me would go out and hunt up some character, the bigger the better, and ajitate a fight between me and him.

We'd go out there and fight. Lots of times, I'd be beat half to death and I'd just keep on going, just like always, I wouldn't quit. Don't reckon I had sense enough to quit. I guess they laid down bets on us, as to which one of us would win.

I finally caught on to the situation, and I started going after the ones that was a doing the ajitating and that soon put a stop to it. Anyhow, I done alright. I know it was because I had to fend for myself from the time I was big enough.

They buzzed our hair off during basic training. I didn't much care for that but they done it to everybody. I liked my thick, wavy hair. Didn't much like the buzz. But I think they done it in case any of us had lice, so they could get shed of them first-off.

I had a lot of trouble with basic training, close order drill and that sort of thing. I wasn't to dad-gone smart, you know, what with not having much education and book learning. But I made up for it in a lot of other ways and managed to gain the other guys respect.

I could enter a training situation and I'd always come out on top of ever dad-burn thing we done.

We had close order drill to teach discipline as a unit. We worked sun up to sun down. We done gun drills—that's learning to detail strip and name each part---tell what part it played, machine guns or rifles. I liked the machine guns. They were impressive.

We had field maneuvers a lot of times at two a.m. in the morning and it pouring the rain. That was to toughen us up but it sure made us miserable.

We done push-ups by the skillion. We had to run five miles out and five miles back in all kinds of weather and at all times of the day and night. They wanted to be sure we could handle what lay ahead.

We had six weeks of basic training. The things that I had already gone through made it a lot easier for me than some of the rest. I was secretly sorry for some of them. You couldn't be in this man's army and be a softie so nobody knowed it.

I finally settled in till I was more or less a normal person like most of the men in there.

I went from Fort Thomas to Fort Knox and from there to Fort Custer, Michigan for maneuvers and stayed there nine months. I began to put on a little weight, being fed regular. 'Fore I went on into the real war, I had gained up to one hundred and eighty five pounds. I wasn't fat by no means but heavier than I'd ever been in my life. I was healthy and still muscular and I know muscles weigh more than fat. Don't reckon I could ever have been called fat. Wasn't in my constitution to run to fat, just plain to stringy, I was.

When you had trained up and was ready, you went on maneuvers. At revelie, we'd fall out, which was six a.m. They divided us up into two parts, one group blue, one red, and one group held the hill, the others tried to take it. There was referees in the war games.

The full field pack weighed a full thirty five pounds. I had trained for the position of machine gunner and the machine gun tri-pod weighed in at fifty-one pounds. I had to carry both the field pack and the tri-pod. My partner carried the business end of the machine gun. I done a lot of target practice 'cause an expert got paid extra. We was paid twenty one dollars a month and you got five dollars extra if you was a gunner, or an infantry man and five dollars more for combat.

We trained under live fire. There was barbed wire a foot off the ground and we had to crawl under it. We made sure to stay on the ground for to rise up was deadly. I had to drag my machine gun and when I set it up, it could turn left and right but not up and down.

We carried c-rations for eats, including corned beef hash or pork and beans.

At night time, lights were out at nine o'clock. If we had to go to the restroom, we went in the dark. If anyone went home without asking, they had gone AWOL.

What I was going to get to here, is down to the nitty-gritty. I went into the service in 1940 and in 1942, we went overseas. I stayed in the service for five and a half years. If you was drafted, it was for three years, or I guess till you was injured bad or killed one.

When you joined up, you joined for the duration of the war.(or till you was injured bad or killed one) It was so different to anything I ever experienced before in my life and I had a lot of living experience under my belt. I had a strong survival instinct, too, from where I'd fended for myself for so long. I knowed how to take orders but I knowed how to take care of myself, too.

We already had a lot of basic training, went on a lot of manuvers and done a lot of war training and all that. Maybe I should just get to it right now and tell some of the outstanding things that happened, some of the things that went on during manuvers. You may not find them all that interesting but to us that lived to tell about it, it was. AND you actually just MIGHT find it interesting.

When we'd come in of an evening after a hard day of training, we'd be real tired but we'd spread a blanket over the grass and play poker. This was while we was still training for battle. Four or five or six of us'd gather up around that blanket a playing cards. One old guy, he was up on his knees and another one, he was setting down right straight across the blanket from that first one.

Them two got into an argument and the one that was on his knees, he just jumped straight up through the air and hit that guy full in the face and killed that other guy deader than four o'clock.

They took that old boy away and worked with him a long time trying to get him back but we found out later that he died. Things like that happened.

Another time, this guy flopped down on his back and went to asleep outside. Been out all night the night before, I guess. Anyhow, he's a laying there asleep with his mouth wide open. People passed by him right and left, ignoring him. But this one guy comes up, gets down on his knees in front of the sleeping man and takes his ding-dong out, runs his finger through the guys mouth and ....well.....you can guess what happened next.

That sleeping man woke up and realized what was going on, I guess he sobered up fast 'cause he jumped up from there and knocked that other feller on his keister. He went straight backwards and landed flat on his back. They come and took him away on a stretcher. I don't know what happened to him but the other guy went a gagging off. But things like that....well....they happened.

We were shipped off to Indiantown Gap, PA, with a short lay-over then sent on to New York Harbor. We loaded on a ship there and it was two days before take-off. The troops went in a convoy with planes escorting the convoy over. We arrived in Iceland in May of 1942 and spent nine months there. That sure was a miserable place up there. It was to cold to train or do manuvers of any kind there.

We was rationed six cans of beer a week. Didn't have to pay for it, they just issued it to us. Didn't have no PX, no store where you could buy nothing so money wasn't worth a durn. We'd play poker, each can of beer would buy so many poker chips. We'd put them all in a pile there and we'd play poker for the beer. Man! We had some of the dad-gonedest poker games ever was.

They'd steal cards and everything else. Slip them up their sleeves....Man alive, they wanted that beer. Six cans wasn't gonna do ye much good and everybody was wanting to get drunk, I guess.

That was very nearly the most miserable place ever was. It stayed daylight six months and dark six months. They called it the Land of the Midnight Sun. Really, it is. The river went into salt water and in the winter, the wind was so cold that it would blow the ice up off the water in sheets and freeze the river dry. It was a purty sight but the cold was deadly.

We had lines tied from building to building to hold onto to get to the restroom and mess tent where we ate at. If we didn't hang on to it and there was a blizzard, well, we could get lost real quick and freeze to death. We nearly froze to death anyhow, it was so cold there. I never seen nothing like it before or since. Some days it was to cold to even get out.

One reason we were there was to guard the shore line there 'cause them Icelanders, their chief occupation was fishing. Then they'd go out in them boats and re-fuel German submarines. So every time one of them boats went out, three G.I.'s would go with them. They had to have oil on board to re-fuel the ship and the G.I.'s would go with them and make sure they didn't just go out and re-fuel the sub's, then just come back in. That's what we were there for, that's what I understood anyhow, that's what we done. Another thing we done was to try and build an airport.

We stayed there seemed like forever, and then went to the British Isles, England in August of 1943. It was rainy, windy and warm. Man! What a change! It was a shock to all our systems, I think. But I appreciated the warmth so much.

We stayed there a while then went on to Ireland. We done some manuvers over there, went on lots of hikes, trained and had war games. I made friends with some of the soldier boys there. I even found me a girl there and went courting some. I rode a bicycle over to see her. But I knowed better than to get to close to her 'cause I knowed we'd be a leaving out 'fore long. But there was a lot pretty girls there.

Chapter 7

Finally, France

We did leave, we went back to England. From there we went to France in July of 1944. It wasn't just hop from here to there but it's hard to tell about every thing that happened in every place. A lot of different things did happen where ever we were. We were soldiers far from home and family.

But we were all in the same boat, a lot of us just kids who had never been in combat before. Sure, we had trained even under live fire but that was a different situation entirely. That was friendly fire. These people here really wanted us out of the way, however they had to get rid of us, preferably dead so we couldn't kill none of them.

Now we had to sorter be like that little lizard, the chameleon, they change colors to camouflage themselves against their enemies and to adapt to their surroundings. We had to try to do that. Not so much to change colors as to try to adapt to these new surroundings.

When we got into France, first thing we done was get rid of our gas masks, and packs, everything we possibly could shuck off, we did. We was give a shovel to hang on our belts to dig in with and a spoon to eat with. Time they got to me, they had me one broke spoon. I took care of it. I'd been in this shape before and worse. I knowed the value of any kind of a spoon, even a broke one.

We went into Pattons third Army. We went straight into….. just behind the front lines. The enemy had secured a mile and a half of beach already tied down. We got pinned down first thing. This is where all hell broke loose. This is it! This is what we had trained so hard for. Are we ready? We dad-blamed well better be…..

Our enemy were in attack mode, small deadly men in brown uniforms, some with rifles, others with machine guns, such as myself, some of their suntanned faces hard from the battles they'd already fought, some just boys, first-timers in battle like a lot of us.

Still, they were unorganized so we dug in and waited till everything was ready and when it was ready we made our attack. We never let up. We had quite a bit of trouble getting them on the run, took us two or three days but once we did, we kept them that way. Brown uniforms would emerge fireing from the bushes and we'd send them, reeling back into the bushes, dead as four o'clock.

We were stunned by the screaming, men fighting and dying all around us, the explosions, pounding artillery, clanking tank treads and choking smoke. I cranked up my .30 caliber machine gun and hammered away before they could get me. And it made us all see……..we are ready……we can do it…..

The thunder of war was loud and clear, the heavy fire of enemy tanks and mortars, mixed in with our own tanks and mortars. It didn't even seem real, more like we were having a bad nightmare, so we were sorter able to do our duty and almost dis-associate ourselves from the business of killing. Plain and simple, it was kill or be killed.

And I wasn't ready to die yet. I've already survived to much in my young life to lose my life here….I still had me some dad-burn living to do, if I ever got out of this mans Army and this miserable, stinking war. What-ever it takes…I'm a gonna do it to survive……

During the war, we got K-rations to carry with us. It come in a little box and had cigarettes, matches, instant coffee, chocolate, crackers, peanut butter, and instant 'taters. We were careful lighting up our cigarettes. Never, never let the light be seen by the enemy.

We'd shield it with our whole bodies so close that the end of the cig is all that seen the match. Then we had to shield the burning end so you couldn't see the glow. Being lit up in the dark, even by the glow of a burning cigarette, was a good way to get yourself shot and killed, especially at night. I'm not sure their snipers ever slept.

The higher ups would send out a division including a medical unit and five companies consisting of headquarters, heavy weapons, (two big guns per company) split up in two sections, and three rifle companies (ten riflemen per company) Two companies would be sent on ahead. One company would be held in reserve. Sometimes they'd send out two divisions.

The medical unit was just behind the front lines, setting up a hospital of sorts for the many wounded. It was a make-do situation but it sure beat nothing all to pieces.

Well, now we was in hedgerow country in France. The enemy set up defensive positions in behind them hedge rows. They were stubborn as we were and didn't want to give up an inch. But their strategy was to set up behind them hedge rows, now not ever one, they'd just set up ever now and then. There'd be three or four that you had to go over, and you never knowed which one they was behind. That way it kept us in suspence.

They'd have two or three men up in trees as snipers to pick us off one by one or till we got them. Our men fell beside us all along the way 'till we were able to pick off the snipers. Then after they had fallen, more would come and take their place.

When dark come, everything would mostly stop and when morning come, it'd start all over again. At dark, we'd dig in, stay right there and wait for daylight. We had to be careful to stay down in our foxhole. Stick your head out is a good way to get it shot off. This wasn't no war games or training. This was the real thing. Training seemed very far away right now.

Sometimes during the night, our bowels had to move and we'd carefully dig out a little hole, and making sure we stayed down, wiggle around till we could go in it. We'd take our foot and cover it up with dirt as best as we could but if we moved around much, we'd get in it and we'd be the awfulest stinking mess in the morning. We couldn't help it. When nature calls, you have to do something.

We wouldn't get clean clothes but once ever two or three weeks so we just had to wear it and stink till we did get clean ones but they didn't stay clean long. Every body was in the same shape so thats how it was. We just tolerated the stench 'cause that's all we could do.

We got a hot meal every two or three weeks along with the clean clothes. In between, we got the K-rations. There would be six carriers come ever so often. Four carried ammo and two carried rations and cigarettes. These men sorter was our life-lines. We depended heavily on them for our shells and our food.

At daylight, we'd go on from hedge row to hedge row. This hedge-row country was absolutely THE most miserable part of the whole dad-gone time I was there 'cause we had to watch every second, while we was going from hedge row to hedge row, we expected hell to break loose any minute. We could never let down our guard. Never....

It didn't happen, we went on to the next hedge row expecting it to break loose…and it didn't happen. Walk all day long. Maybe go ten or twelve hedge rows, not get shot at……..

Them farmers used them hedge rows for fencing to keep their stock in. They'd pile up a big pile of dirt, then plant them hedges on top of it. They had a fence when them hedges got started good. I guess that'd been going on for a hundred years for them hedge rows was real big, been there for a long while. Plenty of room underneath them hedgerows for a soldier to dig out a great big hole, bigger enough to hide in, for an ambush.

The most nerve wracking, strangest part of the whole dad-burn war was right in them awful hedge rows. We'd go maybe all day long without getting any resistance and sometimes even two days. That give them plenty of time to dig in real good and hollow out underneath them hedge rows on the other side. They'd just leave a little hole big enough to see us out of and for their gun barrel to poke through so they could shoot at us on our side.

They'd wait till we got up right real close and then they'd open up. We'd go along thinking 'is THIS the one? Am I going to get it here? Is THIS the one?' For some of us, it was.

We were always on edge. It wasn't the fact that I was afraid that I was going to die, I wasn't scared, just tensed up, all the time…we all were……just can't be explained. Don't think anybody in the whole world has the words to tell how it was…..you know it's a coming, (chuckle) but you don't know which hedge row it's coming from. That's what made it so miserable. It was so hard on a fellers whole nervous system….it was just a constant…….I'd say….dread…… for lack of better words to explain.

It got to where you just want it to hurry up and happen. You just thought, as you hurried along, 'Dang, let it go ahead and happen, let this hedge row be the one! Let's just get it over with.' I tell you, it was the most miserable.

The front lines was death, hell and destruction. This war would break an iron man. And I wasn't no iron man, contrary to popular belief.

They pushed us back but they wasn't no way they could stop us, they was to dad-gone many of us, wave after wave of us. If we took a field, we held it. When some died, others took their place, some of them to die there. We'd dig in of a night and sometimes they's counter attack and we'd have to fight of a night. We'd always hold on there.

Sometimes they'd manage to get in amongst us. A few of them would make it through but normally we cut them off before they got there. We had tank support, artillary, mortar support and whenever they opened up, we did too. Sometimes it'd go on for hours.

We'd stop of a night and dig in and wait for morning to attack again. We moved forward every dad-gum day. During this time, we'd get our replacements, to replace the dead and the wounded. They'd come in silently of a night to replace them that weren't there no more.

I was number one gunner, I had an assistant gunner always and during the hedgerow situation, I had three different assistant gunners. At first, I'd try to go get aquainted with them guys, you know, find out their names and if they had a family, but I cut that out 'cause you didn't want to get to know nobody you didn't have to. You just never knowed who'd be next.

It kept us under a dad-burn stress and strain all the damn time. You couldn't sleep of a night on account of it. At first, it was very nearly impossible to get any rest....it was a whole lot of difficulty in sleeping. You just laid down where you was after you got dug in, stayed still as you could..

I stayed in the machine gunner position…I had to dig a bigger hole, 'Course I had to get one of them other fellers to help me dig. We'd dig a good gunner place in case we got a counter attack to where the gun would be. We'd dig a hole in a half moon, like, and then dig out in the front of the flat part, about a foot down to where we could set the legs down and the muzzle or barrell, that is, the business end of the thing would be flat clear at the top of the ground. You'd have cover and you'd get grace in fire that-a-way.

Can I tell you how we operated in that way? The machine guns operated in pairs. The effective range on them things was about a thousand yards. Well, we'd set them things up…..One gun was aimed from the left, having it sitting there stationary, in case, to fire to the right of the target.

The machine gun on the right, which would be about sixty feet apart, would fire to the left. That way in which it would give us crossfire in case they came through the field. If they came through the field, they had to come through that crossfire. There was no way they could get through, as long as them machine guns was opened up they…could…NOT…..get through….

So what they'd do when we'd open them dad-gone machine guns up, they'd start raining in mortar fire in on us. We'd have to leave our position and when a shell landed behind you and one in front of you, you was zeroed in, so now you gotta move. We'd move out of our gun position, we'd have a spot already picked out for our fore spot to go to. We'd go to the most convenient one and then while we was even fireing our guns, we'd be a picking out another spot to go to. Had to, only way to survive.

We knowed we couldn't fire but about a half a belt of ammo till they would be raining mortar shells in on us. So we'd have to move again and work our way around and wind up back in the same gun position. We done that a lot.

They'd already zeroed in but they'd already dropped a whole lot of battle fire in that spot. They wasn't set to do it again right away and the strategy we used worked. The strategy we had to use was to save our own skins and be more effective at what we was a doing.

We never got used to the screams of agony, their men and ours. We'd rush out at them, charging the enemies lines with all we had. A few of us died but we got more of them. We had to just jump or step over the dying or dead bodies and go on. Ever way we turned, we saw grisly death, bloody men mangled beyond recognition......We were always aware that it could be one of us, us that was still fighting, a laying there, mouth twisted in death, our lifes blood flowing out on foreign soil.

No time to mourn the dead.....friends, enemies......this was a situation that I'd never been in before. I'd heard some stories of the first World War and what the men had to do to survive....it all become very real to me here.....

Everything had to be done of a night before we settled in to sleep what we could, our ears still ringing from all the artillary fire, bombing and blasting during the day, sometimes low rumbling thunder sounds in the distance and the echos of it, but mostly right beside us, even up in our face. Many of us lost hearing in one or both ears, myself included, in one ear.

Those of us that did survive had many disabilities, both physical and mental. But the guns were usually silent after a long day of combat on both sides, a strange kind of uneasy quiet. I guess just knowing they were out there and we would start all over at the beginning of a new day.

The noncommissioned officers would gather in a spot of a night and plan out the next days strategy. They'd pick out on the map the next days objective to accomplish.

They'd pick out a land block that we could see, that we'd seen the evening before anyhow, that was them guys durn job, and they'd pick out objectives for a particlar unit to accomplish the next day. Most of the time we succeeded in what ever they had planned out. They knew we would (or die trying).

They'd come around, after they had the next day all figured out, and tell me, then go tell the other gunner on the other gun. The squad leaders of the rifle companys would be informed. The word would be passed along untill everybody knew it or had a general idea what they was gonna try to accomplish.

Sometimes we couldn't do it right away, there was to much resistance. But we'd make the effort and maybe it'd take us two days to do it, but we'd eventually do it. We'd dig in of a night and lay down where we were and have our night-mared dreams. Not much rest at all.

We'd wake up breathing hard and sweating from the nightmares, and then, try to calm our racing hearts by breathing dusty air in and out as slow as we could, as we tried to clear our heads of the horrible combat images in our night-mare induced minds. We were aware, even in our sleep that we dared not set up. We knew to do that was to get our heads blown off.

Knowing tomorrow would be the same as today. The days were more a nightmare than the nights because the bloody, horribleness that passed in front of our eyes was real.. I say we, 'cause I know the others in my outfit had the same problems as I did with it. I had lost a lot of weight and couldn't hardly keep my fatigues up on my thin body. Getting poor and stringy again, I was. I guess it was the constant nervous energy that burned up more than what I had to eat.

I thought we'd NEVER get through them dad-burn hedge rows but we finally did. We got into a different area…a different type of situation…..and then things changed, the strategy and the type of terrian changed considerably.

The war was heating up more and more ever day. It was getting much worse and harder and harder to accomplish what we set out to do. They was just as determined as we was.

One particular time, we was assigned to take a hill that was visable, they picked it out and we could see where it was----We was to take the top of that mountain and establish the high ground for an outpost…you know…an observation post. Well, it wasn't all that easy. The enemy had dug in real good and halfway up the hill, that's what they'd done there, too.

They were very heavily armed both places with heavy mortar artillary, both big and small tanks, scattered around a waiting. They'd wait untill we got right up to the foot of the mountain, then they'd open up. I had to crawl on my belly and drag that dad-burn machine gun equipment, keeping up with everybody else, till I got ready to set it up.

Me and my assisant gunner could set the thing up in six seconds flat. He carried the business end of the gun and I carried the tri-pod.

When I started adjusting the legs on that tri-pod, my assistant would run up there and put the gun on it. He wouldn't be very far behind me, I mean he stuck real close to me. I'd get that gun belt out of the box, that is if I needed another belt in it. Sometimes it already had a belt in it. I'd lock it in and open up. I'd fire about one fourth or one half a belt. The belt held two hundred and fifty rounds and ever sixth round was a tracer, that's the way they loaded them belts and you could see what you was a hitting and where ye bullet was a going.

This particular time, we couldn't make it. They pinned us down and then they got into a tank battle right there. Them tanks come a charging out of them trees and we had tanks in front of us, behind us, the battle was loud, fast and furious.

During them times, we just laid back there, heck! There wasn't nothing for us to shoot at. We just watched that tank battle go on. We got to watch things like that a lot. Them dad-gone tanks'd be out there just a shooting the dickens out of each other.

I can't remember ary a time we was stopped for long because of it 'cause as you well know, we won. Our tanks beat theirs. We'd wait till it was all over with 'cause they'd always keep a few tanks back for the infantry men. We'd call those in purty quick.

We'd just lay and wait till it was over with. Once it was, we'd go on about our business. The tanks they'd kept back to stop us didn't do it, we kept on a going.

Chapter 8

The War, As I Saw It

If you have a queasy stomach, you might want to skip a few pages. If you're of strong constitution, you thats reading this book, then read on.

One time there was a road that was cut through a gap that was neck high. If you was in this road, there was a bank on each side of you. We were under heavy shelling and trying to get out of the line of fire. There was a whole bunch of us guys running down this gap, myself included. I was a running down through there hard as I could go and there was a guy laying there with his head a laying back. I skidded to a stop and looked at him. I NEVER will forget this...I still have nightmares about it now. There was about a half inch of flesh holding his head on his shoulders.

I stared at him but I didn't see NO blood, I tell you, there wasn't a drop of blood.and the man decapitated. It had just this minute happened for his mouth was wide open and he was gasping for air, still trying to breathe. I was just there a few seconds but I got myself an eyefull. The look on his face was pure awful, shocked horrible......Ah! Dang! I wish I hadn't of seen it. If I knowed the guy, I didn't recognize him. I could have known him....I don't know. Things like that happened over there all the time but this one is especially strong in my memory.

What puzzled me about it then and I still can't figure it out now, is how come there wasn't no blood. I guess schrapnel had hit him, the shell had probably landed right on the bank, neck high and just took his head off. It had closed the veins and arteries off as it went, is the only thing I can figure. Seared and sealed them together as it went through his neck.

Anyhow, I wish I hadn't of seen that or what happened next, either one. I looked back after I got up the road a piece and I saw a tank come rumbling along and run right over the guy. I know it did 'cause I was looking. I couldn't help looking back. That tank for sure run over him. I heard the brittle, crunching sounds of bones breaking. It squashed him all to pieces but he was already dead and that's for sure. I couldn't believe what my eyes had just seen.

Well, that's just one of them damn miserable incidents of which there was several. But that was one of the worst ones. It still squinches up my insides when I even think about it. It's hard to tell you about it. It brings up long shoved back memories that haunt me to this day. I know I'm not the only one. Every soldier has a story to tell. But some prefer not to, it's just to painful for some of us to bring up the horribleness of the war and our friends getting blown up right beside us.

Why did they have to die and I got to live? Was it just luck or a higher power that saved us? Why was I one of the lucky ones? Was... I.... one of the lucky ones.... by surviving? I sure don't know the answer to that one....

The veterans of World War II are leaving this old world at an alarming rate. Going to their eternal reward. There has to be a special reward beyond this life for the ones that lived through the horrors of war and made it back home, don't they? We have to tell our story or it wont get told. It will be forever silenced when we are all gone. That's why I want to tell you what I saw and what happened to me. So you'll know.

So when you see a veteran with his head held high, you'll maybe actually give thanks that he left his homeland and protected it in the only way he knew how, in the way he was trained to do. So you can live free the way you do now. Maybe you'll feel a little more respect for him than you ever have before. Maybe you might actually want to shake his or her hand.

Can I tell you about another incident that I witnessed there that I wish I hadn't? I was just a sitting….I don't know what occasion it was or what situation. We was held up for a while or something. I was looking up at the sky at a small Piper Cub plane. They used them for artillary observers, spotters to direct artillary. They flew them little planes up there where they could see more fronts.

Anyhow, that guy must have been flying to low. I just happened to be sitting there looking up at that plane a flying around there and all at once, KABOOM! That plane just disentergrated. He's supposed to direct artillary for them and them two forty artillary pieces.

Anyhow, he was probably flying to low and one of them hit him. I watched as the wing of the plane just folded around and the engine part of it just come straight down. The rest of it exploded into large pieces like parade confetti and floated down. I set there sort of in shock and watched that plane…. Slowly…..slowly…..float…. down….. to… the ground. I thought, 'My God! There was a MAN in that!'

Another time, almost under the same circumstances, I was just looking up the road at a little bitty tank. It was hauling the dickens, what I mean is, he was just a flying down the road. He stopped dead sudden and he went right straight up in the air about twenty feet.

He'd got on a mine, I guess, but what was puzzling to me about it was how straight up in the air he went.

And I was looking right straight at it. If I had blinked I would have missed it. That is, except for the after-effects. You got on a mine in one of them things, you just plain didn't have a chance.

I seen a whole load of dad-gum crap but I guess everybody else that was in the war did, too. We all saw different incidents but purty much all the same, I guess. Different situations, but these are just some of the ones I saw. I still think about it to this day, I can't help it. You can't never really get it off your mind. I guess that's the way it is with all of us.

It is, you might say, sorter ingrained in our conscious mind and our sub-conscious, too. We saw it with our own two eyes. It's there, it's always there, always just in the back of your mind, and sometimes lurking around in the front, ready to get you. Never far from your thoughts. You cant NEVER get over it.

The children that suffered over this mans war was another situation that I hated. A lot of them was left to fend for themselves in the streets. I been there, done that. One time one little feller, about five or six years old, that we was well aquainted with, jumped on a mortar shell that hadn't exploded. Some of them was duds, you know. This one wasn't, but it hadn't exploded before for reasons I'll never know. I guess the boy must have twisted it just right but however it happened, it exploded as he fell and blew one leg clean off. Now there was a lot of blood here.

That little boy was grabbed up and carried out of there but the two men that took him come back in real soon. They was both crying.

One of them said, wipeing his handkerchief across his face, " He didn't even live to get to the top of the hill."

Done any good, I'd a cried, too and you know I don't cry. But I thought a lot of that little boy, I couldn't help it. I'd shared my food with him, many times before. He had gumption like myself when I was that age.

Man! It's been sixty two years and….I….still….have…. nightmares……about ……situations….like……that. Not as often as I did when it first happened but way to often to suit me.

Chapter 9

Germany

I'll tell you about another incident that still brings chills to my bones. We got into the border of Germany on the Mosaic River. We pulled up into a little old town overlooking the river. The enemy started shelling the town, they just tore it all to pieces.

We was right at the river and we was going to cross it. We was assigned to take a mountain over there. They sent two machine gun squads across the river, on pontoon boats, (rubber boats). I was sent with this bunch.

Now this mountain was kindly out to itself, none to the left and none to the right, just the one mountain peak. It was like you'd draw a picture of a dome, out on level ground and we was to take control of that. We went carefully on our way. We'd seen worse, we'd done worse, we'd took control of worse. We expected to take control of this. Didn't look to bad.

We headed across the river, we never got shot at....there wasn't no fire opened up or nothing. Just deadly quiet. Raise the hair up on the back of our necks is what it did. You know, just knowing something aint right.

We went on across, unloaded, and got started toward that mountain. It was about a mile inland after you cross the river. Yep, about a mile to this durn mountain peak that I'm a talking about. I don't know where you'd call it a peak or what….it was just kindly off to itself. No other mountain like it anywheres near it.

The reason they had sent us across the Mosiac river when they did was called a tactic. While we was a going over there across the river, them others went up the river about six miles and laid a pontoon bridge and crossed big fashion. While we was a drawing fire over there, they was making a big plunge.

This is how Patton operated. He sent a small unit on ahead to draw fire and that was the tactics he used. I guess it was good strategy far as he was concerned but it wasn't all that good for most of us. A lot of our men didn't make it.

One time while we was still in England, Patton was supposed to come and make a speech for us. We all loaded up in trucks, four, five and six divisions and gathered up in a big old playground. They had built a platform to accomodate him there. We stood out in the hot sun for a long time, about three hours a waiting for that rascal to show up.

We seen this plane a coming in and landing and knew it was him. He got out and walked up on that platform. He cussed and used all kinds of language for about five minutes, then walked back off the platform and got on his plane and left. Most of us, myself included, were not impressed. Sorter dumb-founded, we was.

Ah! I was a telling about that mountain……..We started going up that durn mountain, making our way, watching, extra careful. We got plumb up to the top and here was a fort setting on the very top of the mountain! They had a BIG old gun that….God…you could drive a jeep in the barrell of it. It was one of them short stubby ones….I know you've seen pictures of it on television. It was just setting there looking ominous. They had it rigged to where they could bring it up on the elevator out of this here fort on top of this knoll and fire up a storm, then let it back down in there.

Well, we got right up there to where we could see it. The lieutenant was right behind me. He was the platoon leader and soon as he seen it, he took off a running back over the hill hard as he could go. I did, too, in fact, we all did, we all run down that damn mountain. I looked around behind us after he done already started running and I didn't see nobody.

I thought, 'What the hell? They may not be nobody in that thing, they may not be nobody there!'

We never seen nobody but when we got back down to the foot of the mountain and headed towards the river, then we seen what they'd done. They'd come in behind us, while we was a going up the mountain, they'd cut us off from the river. So THAT'S where everybody was. Then they started shooting at us from the durn river AND the top of the mountain. They had us pinned in between the mountain knoll and the river. They had pinned us down good. We really was between a rock and a hard place now.

The lieutenant got shot through the fleshy part of his leg coming off the mountain. He went off to his-self and bound it up. An aide man was there and was a gonna fix it for him but he wouldn't let him, he fixed it his-self.

I was sitting there a watching him and he called in a radio man, they had sent a radio man in there with us, and he called in OUR artillary. They started dropping shells right in on top of us. Now that was NO fun at all......shells exploding all around us and from our own army, too. The lieutenent was quick to call and cancel it out. They stopped shelling after a few minutes. We stayed pinned down three days and three nights. Wasn't no way we could get back to the dad-burn river.

There was just two squads of machine guns is all they was. We didn't have any rifle support. We fit them off anyhow…we set up a position on each flank and according to the Stars and Stripes, I found out later on that we beat off twenty six counter attacks a trying to overcome our two machine gun squads AND we held out three days and three nights.

We finally fought our way back down to the river and we put our equipment in the river. We waited 'till about midnight and then we dumped our guns, all our guns and everything else in the river. We had one guy there that couldn't swim, his name was Burton and I never will forget this character. I was setting on the bank a talking to him after I'd done dumped my gun in the river. I was fixing to hit the water and start swimming.

I said, "I'm a going.…..come on, lets go, Burton."

He said quietly, " I can't swim!"

I said, "Man, what are ye gonna do?"

He answered, "I'll just set here."

One guy overheard the conversation and spoke quickly to him, " Do ye want me to stay here with ye? I will, if ye want me to."

Burton answered, " Nah, you go on, I'll just stay here by myself."

So he did. I dove in and swam away and so did the others. I don't know what the hell ever happened to Burton.

What's so strange about this, the day before, this guy Burton had come up to me and said, " I want to give ye my pocket watch to keep to give to my daddy, in case anything happens to me. It's his watch."

I said, " Why, hell, I dont want ye watch.…..(chuckle)….you know I aint……damn!…you got just as good a chance as I have!"

And that kindly struck me as odd. But I didn't take it. Well, anyway, this IS odd. Allow me to fast forward for just a minute or two. Several years after the war, I got a job at Fridgedare and I was working with a bunch of women. I was running a press and the women was doing the wiring...........and one of the women's name was Burton.

I asked her, "What's ye husband work at?"

She replied, "Oh, my husband got killed in the war."

I said, "What'd ye say ye name is?"

She said, "Burton." She was looking at me oddly.

I already knew her name but I guess I just wanted her to confirm it. I got to talking to this woman and it WAS this guys wife that I had been in the war with. If I had only taken the watch, I could have given it to her. I wisht that I had took it.

I had just started telling her about that night when she started crying. Just a sobbing her heart out so I quit, shut my mouth up right quick.

I was gonna tell her the whole story, how I was with him there and tried to get him to come with me, how I didn't really know but maybe he had undertook to swim that river and drowned or else he just set there and the enemy come along and shot him or something. But then I realized that would have been to hard on her, even after all this time. She was already tore all to pieces.

Anyhow, I know it was the same guy 'cause he had the same first, middle and last name. It fit and she knew it when she started crying. I hushed up right quick about it. I seen the foreman the next day and got transferred to another machine. I didn't want to cause the lady any undue stress. I'm sure she had suffered for years anyhow. Strange as the dickens, it was...odd....peculiar.

Rewind back to the dad-gone river...and the field full of artillary fire.

We swum the river and got out of there. That is, some of us did.... some died...some made it....me, I got lost. Everybody was on their own, we didn't have nothing.....we was stripped down far as we could to swim the river. We was supposed to assemble at a certain spot but I didn't know where that spot was. I didn't understand what they was talking about, they didn't have time to tell you anyhow, they was just hollering it to whoever could hear. I couldn't half hear them with all the explosions and shelling going on around me.

Anyhow, during this process of crossing the river, I got hit with schrapnel in the right arm. They had air bursts about the time we got halfway across. The majority of us was still swimming. My arm bled and hurt like the dickens but I never paid it much mind 'cause I was intent on surviving. An artillary shell exploded real close and I lost the hearing in my left ear.

When I got across the river, I didn't know which way to go. Where was everybody anyhow? My head roared like a freight train. There was a big old field there and they was dropping artillary hand over fist in it. I decided instead of going through the dad-gone field where they was dropping so much dad-gone artillary fire, that I'd turn to the right and go around it.

I thought, 'Why, hell, I'll go to the right.'

I come upon a foxhole and then a railroad track that run right parallel with the river. I took off down the railroad track. I knowed about railroad tracks. They take you places. I was gonna go till I got to the right of where they was dropping all the artillary and then cut left and go around all the artillary fire.

Then I started thinking, 'I better get off this railroad track.'

It wasn't all that dark and I could be seen clear as day from the other side of the river. It was swampy, it had been raining and there was a lot of puddles, mud holes. So I got on the other side of the railroad tracks that was over on the swampy side. Didn't care how muddy I got, I already was anyhow, long as I wasn't seen and shot.

Shells were exploding everywhere. So I got down on my belly and
crawled along. Caught my foot on a pinball home-made grenade and
it exploded, sending some shrapnel directly into my leg. Now I had
one bum arm and a bum leg. I was bleeding from both.

I crawled on a while and I heard somebody talking, then they was
real quite. I kept on a listening as best as I could with my good ear
and I could tell they was a speaking English.

I thought, "Damn! I got it made!"

And sure enough I did. But I liked to of got shot by my own side.
Wouldn't that have been a heck-of-a note? Stuff like that happened,
though. It sure did. There was a sentry there, and he told me
afterwards, I didn't know it at the time, that he was ready to lay it on
me. I stood up and hollered. I guess that's the only reason that I'm here
relating this story now, that's all that kept the guy from shooting me.

Anyhow, just before this, I had got hit with schrapnel in the
right arm, too. When I run into these guys, why, they stopped the
bleeding, bandaged my arm and my leg up and fixed it for me. I went
with them, they left out of there right after daylight.

That feller told me, the captain there, he said, "You go up this hill
here and turn to the left and you'll find yer outfit."

I said, " I aint got no weapon or nothing, sir."

He went and got a rifle and give it to me. I went up the hill and
found my unit. Well, that very same day, ever one of us that made it
back in, and there was precious few of us, they sent us to an evacuation
hospital. It was a big old tent they had stretched away out there.

I guess there was about fifteen of us a laying out on the grass,
asleep there for I don't know how long, we was so dad-burn tired. I
opened my eyes and a guy was standing over me with a clipboard in
his hand a writeing on it. I rared up and set on up and started talking
to him, fireing questions at him.

"How'd we make it here? How long have we been here? How many of us made it?"

He just ignored me and headed over to the next guy and I demanded, " Where we going from here?"

He looked back over his shoulder at me and answered, wearily, " You're Z-I'd."

I didn't know what he was a talking about and here's how he explained it to me. It meant Zone of Interior. It was December 1944. It meant the war was over for me but the war wasn't offically over till September 30th, 1945. That was it for me, though. I'd soon be going home to the good old U.S of A. Relief was so great, flooding my whole being. But I couldn't relax.

Once you've been through what we'd just been through, there just aint no way to get calm. Nerves had carried me through all the miserys of war. Nerves would be at work from now on.

When the war was finally officially over, I was so happy at the time. No more killing.

When they sent all of us to the hospital that had made it across the Mosaic river, I seen Patton again. He come in there a telling us what a good job we'd done and cussed up a storm and left. That's the only times I ever seen the man. And that's the truth. They claimed he was right up front with the troops, well, I was there, and I never seen him. I've talked to others that was there and they never seen him either.

I seen that show, the story of Patton. It showed him out there a directing traffic and all that kind of crap and that's a bunch of bull. Of course, I know……. that guy, he done a good job 'cause we won the war.….only way he knowed to do it, I reckon..…..but at our expence, is the way I see it. Damn! But I guess it was necessary, if it accomplished the purpose. I guess he had to make some awful hard decisions. Sacrifice some, in order to get the job done. Keep the wheel a turning. It turned…it sure did turn….

Then President Roosevelt died in office in April of 1945. Truman replaced him.

Chapter 10

Conclusion (I'm going home!)

I was sent back home to recuperate. I'm a fairly fast healer, didn't take me to long. I rode the Queen Mary ship home to New York, to a Long Island hospital for a week then was sent on to a hospital in Camp Atterbury, Indiana. I was honorably discharged from the Army at Wright Patterson Air Force Base on October 31st, 1945. From there I rode a bus home.

I was in the Normandy Campaign, the Germany Campaign, and the Northern France Campaign. From these services, I received Three Bronze Service Stars, the American Defense Service Medal, the Good Conduct Medal, Expert Infantry Medal, Combat Infantry Medal, EAME Theater Medal, and a Purple Heart. My military occupational specialty was Machine Gunner but I was also M rifle Expert, Pistol 45 Expert and 30 Cal Machine Gun Expert.

I was actually in the service for four years, eight months and twenty six days. Two years, eight months and twenty days of this time was spent in foreign service. I was in Iceland in 1942, the British Isles in 1943 and France in 1944. I was with Company H, 11th infantry, my APO 209. The highest grade that I held was Pfc, Private First Class. It says on my Honorable Discharge paper that I went through eight years grammer school. I must of stretched that a bit or they did one.

I guess I was one of the lucky ones. I made it home.

I had bought me a bunch of new clothes but I forgot my duffel bag with them in it on the bus. I was to excited to be getting home, I suppose. I was still tensed up and plenty nervous, too. But somebody was pleased to find all them new clothes, I bet. Nothing to be done about it though. I just lost them all.

I went back to work in the coal mines in Hazard, Kentucky. I worked there for seven years. I worked seven years insulating refrigerators and from there to the Dayton Steel Foundry in Dayton, Ohio.

I had forgiven my Dad for what he done to my Mom. Had to. That was long over and not a thing to be done about it anyhow. I got over it. And too, I knowed you had to forgive them that done bad things to you. So I did. I got over it and I hoped all my brothers and sisters did, too. Don't bother me no more. I even partnered up with him for a time working.

Soon as I got home though, I went to looking for me a woman to settle down with. I was wanting to find me a real nice girl, get married, have a family, have a home to call my own. Never had a home before to call my own. I'd like to settle and stay put. I'd had enough roaming, rambling, and warring.

I went to my uncle and told him the situation, " Uncle, it's time I found me somebody and settled down. Time I had a family and a place to call my own."

He grinned from ear to ear and said, "I know just exactly who you're looking for, buddy."

He described this girl to me and somebody pointed her out to me at church. God, she was beautiful. I didn't know if she'd want anything to do with the likes of me or not but I went over and set down beside her anyhow. She never protested so I walked her home. A week or two later we was married. We got eight kids now and I don't know how many grand-kids and great grand kids. Soon be SIXTY TWO years we been together. And that's my story.

Mr. And Mrs Irvin Yancey

December 2007
Mrs. Cymbaline Yancey
Pigs and Chickens

I guess everyone has been told how Irvin and I met at the church.
When we got married, what I wore for my wedding blouse was what my
Mom had made me out of pretty flour sacks. I know she made my skirt,
too, out of something she had on hand. I had a flannel boy's shirt that
I wore. It was very much in style at the time. All the girls was wearing
them. I remember I was wearing high heel shoes that my Aunt Grace had
given me. They were hard to walk in. I didn't have any socks.

Aunt Grace is the one who named me when I was born, too. She
read a lot of different books and she had read this Shakespearan play
that had the name Cymbaline in it, only it was a man in the book.
She liked the name so well that she named me Cymbaline.

Mommy didn't go with us to get married on December 19th,
1945. So Irvin and I went to Neon to be married by a Methodist
minister with the minister's wife and son as witnesses. They were
strangers to us. I was young, still in school. Irvin was twenty three
years old, fresh out of the war.

Then we went to a restaurant to eat with a friend of ours. We
went back home and Mommy took Irvin off to the side and told him
he needed to buy me some socks. He did. He sent somebody after

them and they went and bought me some. That made walking some easier in the heels.

We took the last bus to Hazard in a big snow. We visited with Irvin's relatives for a couple of days, then went back up to Whitaker and rented a three room, very poor apartment, downstairs of a neighbor. It was a very cold place. When the wind blew, the linoleum rug would lift up. It probably reminded Irvin of Iceland but I only knew what he told me about that. I just knew he said it was very cold. He didn't tell me much about what all went on during the war. Didn't talk about it much at all.

We cooked on a coal stove and heated the rooms with a fireplace. I kept on going to High School. I was a Senior.

Irvin was real nervous and continued going up and down the hollow all day. Mommie said he would change clothes several times a day. He never received any help, ever, for that nervous condition. The Army never informed him that there was any help available so he didn't know.

His brother Carl come and took up with us and I had to cook and clean after us and him, too, while trying to go to school.

Irvin decided he wanted to raise baby chicks in our bedroom in front of the fireplace. He raised them until they were about grown and then he sold them and made a little money that way.

Our first baby son was born after we had been married about fifteen months. Then we bought an old house that had to have a lot of repairing done on it. Irvin dug us a well and put running water in the kitchen. I was pleased to get that.

Our next son was born thirteen months later. Irvin wasn't home this time for the government had sent after him for a physical examination in Ohio. At that time, you had to hunt Doctors to come to your house to deliver your babies. The cost was about twenty five dollars, which was hard to come by. Over the years, we had eight children.

One time Irvin decided he wanted to raise a hog to kill for meat. He didn't know much about raiseing hogs at the time and it didn't grow off very good.

When the children were young and we were going to kentucky to visit their Grandparents, Irvin would keep on driving, running low on gas.

I'd say, " Irvin, you better stop and get gas!"

He'd say, "Ah, next station."

And he'd always run out of gas and he would have to hitch hike to get some in the gas tank. Lots of times, he would take short cuts and we'd end up lost, sometimes in creekbeds. One time he went over a bridge that was condemned and we couldn't turn back. We had to continue through a field and down a creek bed to find a passable road.

Another time we had been to Kentucky and were going home after we had seen a movie in a small town in Ohio. Suddenly we came up on a railroad crossing all lit up with flashing lights. There was a whole car load of us when Irvin quickly threw on his brakes about a foot from the tracks. No one spoke as we were all dumb founded. The passing train scared me within an inch of my life and made all our heads spin.

The government was constantly sending after him for his physical examinations and also constantly lowering his pension. He worked at odd jobs, most any thing he could find.

He worked at odds and ends jobs but never made much money. The government thought because his hands were rough that he was able to work. His nerves was so bad he couldn't work much although he tried. One time he was out of work and had tried and tried to get work or some kind of help one or the other. There wasn't no jobs nor help nowhere to be found so he decided to try and rob a bank. He was very desperate because he had a growing family and no food for the table. Just before he attempted it, he found a job. He was pleased with that.

We had a big flood in our small town. The waters rose up about three feet. Irvin took a push broom and kept sweeping and pushing the mud and water untill the flood waters slowly went down.

Irvin's sister Gertrude, (she's the one who gave him the hair cut in the picture when he was about eleven years old) lived in Wayne County so we moved there and bought this house here over thirty years ago.

We stayed in Kentucky untill we had four children. Our fourth was a girl. On the night she was born, Irvin was so pleased that he took her to visit every ones house to show her off.

It was hard to keep the kids in shoes so one time Irvin bought the boys shoes and had extra soles put on them. He also had steel put on the heels. You know how boys are, they skated on the wood floors at school and the teacher took the extra soles off because they were wearing the floor out.

The first time we moved to Ohio, Mommie hated to see us take the kids off so bad that we could hear her screaming a long distance away. That was really hard.

Irvin worked for Fridgidare in Dayton, Ohio. He followed this one Frididare down the line all the way and it lasted twenty five years. It was a good one.

He and some friends went to Detroit, Michigan to try to get work. He got a job at an automobile factory but there was no houses for rent. He ended up working in a steel factory. It was so hot in there that he couldn't work long at a time.

A friend taught him how to roof houses and he painted some houses, too. Finally he went to a government place and demanded a job. He told them surely he deserved a job after all the time he had spent at war. He worked as a guard for a while then drove a garbage truck for a while. He had seizures until they finally had to retire him from work.

We live halfway up a mountain on a very steep road and it used to be real rough getting up here in the winter time. One dark snowy night Irvin was walking up the hill from where he had been playing cards down town. He heard some young boys coming down the hill and discussing the grave they had to dig at Elk Springs. Irvin played real quite and just as they got to him, he leaped out at the boys. It like to scared them to death. He was still chuckling when he got in home.

We were walking down the hill one slick time and Irvin had our grandbaby in his arms. His shoes was leather soled and he started in slideing with the baby and couldn't stop. But they wasn't neither one hurt. When she was about six months old, Irvin was carrying her out to the well-house in the summer time. He stepped inside and bumped a miners hat hanging on the wall there.

It was full of hornets or some kind of stinging bees and out they swarmed. He covered the grandbaby with his shirttail and ran as hard as he could go with her to get her to safety. Stings didn't bother him none but it sure would have that little baby. I heated a big kettle of boiling water and took it out there and poured it in that hat on the nest.

Our family all got together playing cards and had real good times, argueing with each other about who was winning. Just wonderful, noisy, family get togethers, getting together to play UNO and enjoy argueing who was winning and kidding about who was loseing. The family enjoyed lots of Holidays.

We used to shovel paths down the road off our hill. We enjoyed doing that. This one time, we each shoveled a path off and back up the hill. The road goes on up the mountain but we only shoveled to our house, which is pretty high up on the side of the mountain. After we got home, icy cold and sweaty, we heard a car coming fast up the hill. It reached the end of our path and spun out, couldn't go any further. It had to turn around and go back off the hill. The people in that car were very disappointed.

We actually enjoyed shoveling the roadway off. Sometimes we walked off the mountain to the store in the snow just to be going. We'd buy maybe a candy bar or something.

Irvin had bad nightmares all his whole life. Sometimes he would hit out in his sleep as if fighting off the enemies of the war. He would hit me sometimes when he was dreaming in his sleep. I had to be careful. I knew he never meant to, it's just that awful war and what he suffered through, that caused the bad dreams.

We were attending Rectors Flat Baptist Church back in 1974 when Brother Harold Pitman was pastor there. Irvin and I were baptised at the same time on October the 27th, 1974 in a indoor baptismal. We received our Baptisimal Certificates on August the 13th, 1975.

Time was closing in on him by July of 2007 and he knew it. The very last time I took him to the cementary to check on our grand-son Joshs grave, which is just in front of our tombstone, there was a big, beautiful, bunch of flowers setting perched right on our burial spot.

Irvin laughed, " Somebody jumped the gun there!"

That's the way he was. Always making a joke out of everything.

That morning on August the sixth, I found him, he just looked so peaceful, I thought he was still sleeping. I slipped out and went to the kitchen to make him some coffee. I hollered at him and he never answered. He liked his coffee real hot so I went in there. I wanted to wake him before his coffee cooled off. When I checked him, I didn't admit to myself that he was gone. I called someone and told them I couldn't wake him up.

He looked like he had just left so peaceful. Just went to sleep and slept on out. I don't remember to much about that time, things around then get sort of hazy.

But I do know he would have been so pleased if he had known, that so many people come to see him at the visitation and funeral. There were lots of people that come and signed the book and a lot of people come that didn't sign the book. We found that out later. He always worried that nobody would show up if something happened to him. There was so many people, so many that we didn't even see them all. He would have been very pleased. We would have had our sixty second anniversary yesterday, December the 19th 2007.

Our children:

Paul Yancey	Leroy Yancey
Gary Yancey	Linda Yancey
Donald Yancey	Debbie Yancey
Kaye Vitatoe	Pam Gregory

YANCEY
IRVIN
JUNE 28 1922
CYMBALINE

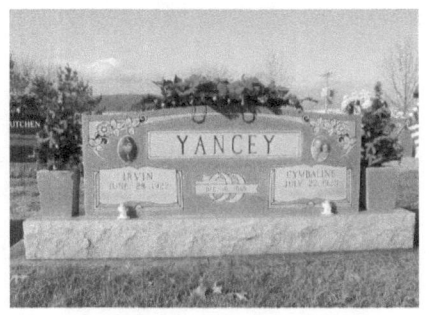

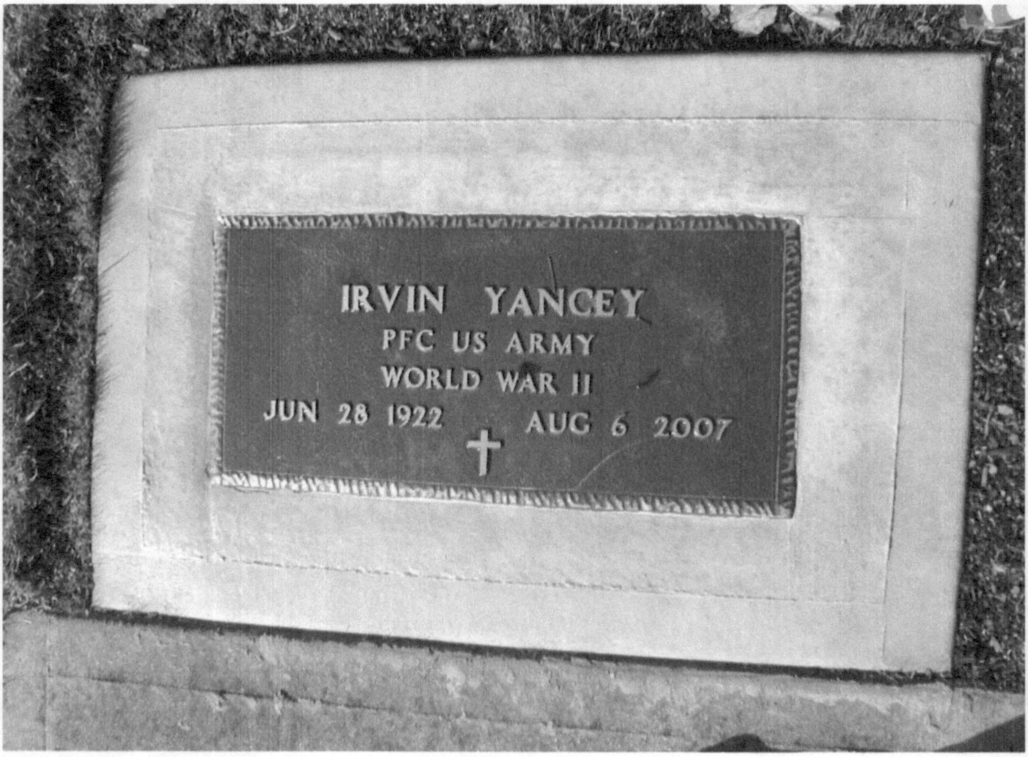
IRVIN YANCEY
PFC US ARMY
WORLD WAR II
JUN 28 1922 AUG 6 2007

In Memory Of All The Brave Soldiers- Those I Knew & Those I Didn"t

Pfc. Irvin Yancey- Army-WWII-Company H--5th Infantry Division
Served 9/27/1940—10/31/1945

Corporal Lyle Criswell—Marines-WWll-1943-1946---Korea—1950-1951

Pfc. Hazel Gregory—WWll—Army

T5 Corporal Drexel Anderson—Navy—WWll- 1945-1947

Pfc.Len Dishman- Army- WWll- 8th Headquarters Calvary- South Pacific

Corporal Carl Bell—Air Force- WWll- 4- 1943- 2-1946

Pfc Shelby Keeton- Army- WWll- 3rd Army, 21st Armored Infantry 11th Armored Division

Sgt. James Patton-Army- WWll- Troupe E- 94th Calvary- 14th Armored Division
Served 5-7-1942—1-7-1946

Pfc. Oather Edwin Baker- Army-WWII-13th tank Battalion- 1st Armored Division 9-1945-7-1946

Pfc Victor C Anderson, Sr. U.S Marines, March-December 1968, Vietnam, Da Nang, Monkey Hill

Staff Sgt. Harold Denney- WWII-603 Tank Destroyer Battalion 1943-1946

Seaman First Class Hershel Slagle-WWII - Navy-3-15-1944—5-1946

Hugh W. Fuller- WWII-U.S. Navy AETM (Aviation Electronic Tech
    Mate) 1-8-42—3-23-47

Robert E. Williams- WWII- U.S. Navy- Machinist Mate 2nd Class-3-
    1942—12-10- 1945

Sgt. Howard Upchurch- WWII- 101st Airborne 6-42—12-45

Sanford Waters- deceased-(my uncle who served in the Army
    WWII-I don't know the dates)

T5 Cpl. Hobert Milton Roberts -WWII-25th Division 1944-1946

Sgt. William D. Crawford- U.S. Army Airforces Air Transport
    Command 12-22-42—12-19-45

Mr. William D. Crawford— Born 6- 21- 1922. My Military
Service is documented in a thick book taken from my collection
of memorabelia and compiled by my daughters. The collection of
orders and government documents, photos, and stories is really
just the story of a country boy who got a letter from Uncle Sam
in 1942 inviting him to report to duty with the U.S. Army. I
left to go into the service three days before Christmas. I received
my honorable discharge and returned home three years later a
few days before Christmas. Many, many incidents happened in
between.

It's just a story of a member of a flight crew's routine. I was very
lucky to get this position and to serve my country. It is not a brag
book. It is all true. We were just an Air Force flight crew doing
whatever was necessary to get the job done that was in front of us. We
handled the unexpected as best as we could under the circumstances.

Our operation up north and across the Atlantic was pioneering
for the air travel that we know today. We didn't know that at the time
of course, but the work the flight crews performed in the war paved

the way for the growth of the flight industry and inventive new air craft for commercial and for military purposes.

With this collection, called <u>Over The Snowball Route 1943-1945</u>, I hope to honor those with whom I served, and those who gave their lives so our nation could stand strong and our families could live in safety and freedom. (5-3-'08)

(Quoted from <u>Over The Snowball Route 1943-1945</u> and reprinted with permission.)

God Bless Our Soldiers, Then and Now

AFTER-EFFECTS

"Being a combat veteran of the Marine Corps is a cost that changes your whole life. I am sixty one years of age and after thirty nine years from combat, I go to see a mental health physican twice a week, sometimes once a week. I take medication three times a day and will have to do so for the rest of my life. I've tried to take my life twice because of intrusive doubts and nightmares. They will never end. It is very true, WAR IS HELL."

Anonymous quote printed with permission.

www.ingramcontent.com/pod-product-compliance
Lightning Source LLC
Chambersburg PA
CBHW020249290526
45784CB00003B/1170